THE PROSE OF OSIP MANDELSTAM

THE PROSE OF OSIP MANDELSTAM

THE NOISE OF TIME
·
THEODOSIA
·
THE EGYPTIAN STAMP

TRANSLATED,
WITH A CRITICAL ESSAY, BY
CLARENCE BROWN

PRINCETON UNIVERSITY PRESS
PRINCETON · NEW JERSEY

Publication of this book has been aided by the
Whitney Darrow Publication Reserve Fund of
Princeton University Press and by the
Research Fund of Princeton University.

Second Printing, with corrections, 1967

Printed in the United States of America
by Princeton University Press, Princeton, New Jersey

Acknowledgments

All students of Osip Mandelstam owe their first debt of gratitude to Professor Gleb Struve and Mr. Boris Filippov, the editors of the *Collected Works*, which appeared in Russian in New York in 1955. The same editors are now collaborating on a much more complete edition in three volumes. For their many unselfish kindnesses to me, and for their interest and encouragement, I owe a further, entirely personal, debt. Professor Struve's scrutiny of certain parts of the translation greatly improved it. For many delightful conversations on the subject of his friend Osip Emilievich I am indebted to Artur Lourié. My colleagues Nina Berberova and Herman Ermolaev have patiently answered many questions, for which I am very grateful. The errors and infelicities which remain are to be blamed solely on my own stubbornness or ignorance. I thank Mrs. Mary Gutbrodt for her kindness in typing parts of the manuscript. For my wife's help in typing the final draft and in reading the proof, and for her other assistance, I am much obliged. I have been greatly aided by some who do not desire public acknowledgment.

Christmas 1964   C.B.
Princeton, N.J.

Note on Second Printing

For many valuable suggestions incorporated in the second printing I am obliged to Simon Karlinsky, Sir Isaiah Berlin, and Donald Fanger.

January 1967   C.B.

A Note on the Transliteration

....

	A	*B*
In the introductory essay and in the translations I have rendered Russian names and titles into Latin letters according to a slightly modified version of the usual scholarly transliteration. This modification is shown in column A. For citing Russian language texts and throughout the notes I have adhered strictly to the scholarly transliteration shown in column B. As usual, exceptions are made for those names like Tchaikovsky, Tolstoy, and Dostoevsky which have grown familiar in another spelling. Non-Russian names appear in their usual orthography: hence, e.g., Rubinstein, Hofmann, and most importantly Mandelstam, which would be Mandel'shtam according to A, and Mandel'štam according to B. When place names contain an adjectival form of a name familiar in English I have used the English form, hence the Nicholas Station, and so on. A foolish consistency in this matter, however, would have produced the Marie Theater instead of the familiar Mariinskij. In quotations from other sources, except where noted, the original transliteration has been changed to conform to the style of this book.

	A	*B*
а	a	a
б	b	b
в	v	v
г	g	g
д	d	d
е	e	e
ё	ë	ë
ж	zh	ž
з	z	z
и	i	i
й	j	j
к	k	k
л	l	l
м	m	m
н	n	n
о	o	o
п	p	p
р	r	r
с	s	s
т	t	t
у	u	u
ф	f	f
х	kh	x
ц	ts	c
ч	ch	č
ш	sh	š
щ	shch	šč
ъ	—	"
ы	y	y
ь	'	'
э	é	é
ю	ju	ju
я	ja	ja

A Note on the Illustrations

Most of the illustrations in this book derive from *Apollon*, a monthly journal of art and literature which appeared in St. Petersburg from 1909 to 1917 under the editorship of the late Sergej Makovskij. Mandelstam's literary debut took place in its pages in the number for July-August 1910.

The border on the title page comes from the cover of the first issue for 1915. The drawing facing p. 3 (from the issue for October 1909) is by Lev Bakst, whose celebrated designs are familiar as a part of Sergej Diaghilev's Ballets Russes. The ornament at the opening of the essay was the tailpiece for Mandelstam's poem "Notre Dame," published in *Apollon*, 3(1913), 38. The drawing of Mandelstam by P. V. Miturich on p. 10 is discussed there. The drawing on p. 13, "Poets," is also by Miturich and also appeared in No. 4-5 for 1916. The title page to "The Noise of Time" (p. 67) is the work of A. Ja. Beloborodov. It appeared in *Apollon*, 2(1913). The design on the title page of "Theodosia" (p. 133) is by V. N. Levitskij and comes from No. 2 for 1913. The design introducing "The Egyptian Stamp" (p. 149) has been redrawn from an engraving by Abragam Bossé which appeared as a frontispiece in the magazine for the year 1911.

The portrait of Valentin Jakovlevich Parnakh on p. 150, discussed on p. 48, is by Pablo Picasso. It appeared for the first time (and, if my search of the Picasso catalogues has been sufficiently thorough, for the only time) as the frontispiece to a book of Parnakh's poems (*Karabkaetsja akrobat*, Paris: Franko-russkaja pečat', 1922).

The rare photographs of Osip Mandelstam and the portrait of him by Lev Bruni (on the jacket) have been kindly supplied by friends to whom I am very grateful. All of these appear here for the first time.

The map of the central portion of St. Petersburg comes from Baedeker's *Russia* (1914), which has remained through war, revolution, and the intervening long time incomparably the best guide to that country. I am grateful to the Karl Baedeker Verlag for permission to reproduce it here.

Contents

....

THE PROSE OF OSIP MANDELSTAM

The Prose of Mandelstam

 The prose which is here offered to the English-speaking reader for the first time is that of a Russian poet. Like the prose of certain other Russian poets who were his contemporaries—Andrej Belyj, Velimir Khlebnikov, Boris Pasternak—it is wholly untypical of ordinary Russian prose and it is remarkably interesting. For reasons that have nothing to do with literature, it is also virtually unknown even, or especially, in Russia itself.

Osip Emilievich Mandelstam, a Jew, was born in Warsaw on the 15th of January, 1891, and died a political prisoner in a camp near Vladivostok in 1938. For years the end of his life was so obscured by rumor, conjecture, and deliberate falsehood that one could be sure only of the fact that he had perished. The date now officially given is 27 December and it is accepted by those close to the event, but there is one rumor left to haunt his biographer and to make it seem the part of prudence to precede the date of 27 December with the bleakly official formula "on or about." Except for details, however, we do seem now to have a large measure of truth about how Mandelstam spent his last days.

His troubles began in 1934. At that time, probably in the apartment of Boris Pasternak, Mandelstam read an epigram which he had written on Stalin. Whether the following excerpt, given here in the English version of George Stuckow, is from the actual poem itself or from another like it is not known, but its authenticity is asserted on good authority, and under the circumstances it is clearly actionable.

> We live unconscious of the country beneath us,
> Our talk cannot be heard ten paces away,

And whenever there is enough for half-a-
    conversation,
The Kremlin highlander is mentioned.
His thick fingers are fat like worms,
His words hit hard like heavy weights,
His cockroach's huge moustaches laugh,
And the tops of his boots shine brightly.[1]

It is unlikely that there were more than five of Mandelstam's close friends within earshot of these verses. One
of them reported the incident to the appropriate authority,
and that was the beginning of the end. Our natural tendency toward revulsion at this act must be tempered by
certain circumstances. The man who did it was himself
in trouble and was probably terrified that one of his associates would show greater and prompter zeal than he,
which would certainly have added to his difficulties. Besides, in a recent work of reference his short biography
concludes with an official cliché which has lately begun to
serve as the laconic epitaph for numerous writers ("Illegally suppressed. Rehabilitated posthumously"), and he perished even earlier than Mandelstam. Requiescat in pace.

The quarter of a century since Mandelstam's death has
not seen him restored to the canon of the elect, though there
have been various signs that his work would be published
again. An announcement in *Voprosy literatury* (Problems
of Literature) for November 1958 (p. 256) declared that
his collected poetry would be published in one of the large
volumes of the distinguished series "Biblioteka poéta"
(Poet's Library), and there were other indications, some
of them very encouraging, that his work would be reissued,
but little has yet come of it. So far as I have been able to
determine, the four poems printed in the almanac *Den'
poézii* (Day of Poetry) for 1962 constitute, with the excep-

---

[1] George Stuckow (pseudonym), "The Fate of Osip Mandelstam,"
Survey, 46 (January 1963), 154f.

tion of isolated quotations, the whole extent of his rehabil-
itation. The bulletin *Novye knigi* (New Books), No. 22
(1964), a prospectus of forthcoming books for the use of
librarians and the book trade, carried the announcement of
an anthology called *Poéty nachala XX veka* (Poets of the
Beginning of the Twentieth Century), scheduled for publication in an edition of 50,000 copies in the fourth quarter
of 1964. Mandelstam is listed along with Bal'mont, Sologub,
Annenskij, Belyj, Kuzmin, Voloshin, Khodasevich, and
other poets for inclusion in this work, which is to be one
of the small-format volumes of the Poet's Library. The announcement names V. N. Orlov, the editor-in-chief of the
entire series, as the editor of the anthology and since that
same Orlov's statement in *Literaturnaja gazeta* (Literary
Gazette) for 27 June 1964 concerning proposed one-volume
editions of Russian poets omits the name of Mandelstam,
it is to be presumed that the long-promised separate collection of his work has been abandoned and that we are
to receive only the few poems which the format and scope
of the forthcoming anthology give one any grounds for
expecting. The formulaic expression mentioned above has
latterly been expanded to read "Illegally suppressed during the period of the cult of personality of Stalin," etc.
Since it was the personal vindictiveness of the dictator himself that caused Mandelstam's tragic death, no one would
seem more eligible for the posthumous amnesty awarded
others. The reason for his continued exclusion is perhaps
one of those curiosities of Soviet internal literary affairs
about which it is seldom very rewarding to speculate.[2]

· II ·

But even non-persons have biographies, though it may be
extraordinarily difficult to establish them. Practically every-

---

[2] As this was being written, the journal *Moskva*, 8 (1964), 143-
152, published a sympathetic memoir of Mandel'stam by Nikolaj
Čukovskij and on pp. 153-155 a selection of eight poems.

thing that we know of Mandelstam's early life comes from his own account in the pages that follow, and the detailed story of his mature years will be the subject of my forthcoming book on his life and poetry. In this introductory essay, therefore, I shall give merely the briefest sketch of his movements from the time of his emergence from the Tenishev School in 1907 at the age of 16 to the time of his death.

Mandelstam went at once to Paris, where, to our immense good fortune, he encountered Mikhail Karpovich (1888-1959), later Professor of Russian Literature at Harvard, who left what is the unique eyewitness account of Mandelstam during his first trip abroad.[3] It is worth quoting at some length:

"This happened in the distant past—nearly a half century ago. I was living in Paris at the time and attending lectures at the Sorbonne. I can give the exact day when I first met Mandelstam: 24 December 1907. As everyone knows, the French celebrate Christmas Eve in the same way that we greet the New Year. On that evening I was also 'making merry' in one of the cafés on the Boul' Miche along with a small group of Russian young people. At a separate table in our vicinity was sitting a certain youth who had attracted our attention by his rather unusual appearance. More than anything else, he looked like a young chicken, and that resemblance gave him a rather comic aspect. But along with that there was in his face and in his beautiful, sad eyes something very attractive. As soon as he heard that we were speaking Russian he became interested in us. It was clear that in the midst of the loud celebration going on about him he felt lost and alone. We invited him to join us and he agreed with obvious pleasure.

[3] "Moë znakomstvo s Mandel'štamom" [My Acquaintance with Mandel'štam], *Novyj Žurnal* [The New Review], 49 (1957), 258-261.

Mandelstam *circa* 1910

Mandelstam *circa* 1936

We learned that his name was Osip Emilievich Mandelstam.

"I was struck most of all by his extraordinary impressionability. It seemed that for him 'all the impressions of existence' were still really new, and to each of them he responded with his entire being. At that time he was filled with a youthful effusiveness and romantic enthusiasm which are difficult to reconcile with his later poetic character. In the future author of *Kamen'* (Stone) there was as yet nothing stony."

For all his ingrained habit of autobiography, Mandelstam was extremely uncommunicative about his family. Though there are, here and there, isolated portraits of individual relatives, there is nowhere in his published writings the slightest hint of what were the relationships among these people. Hence the value of Karpovich's observations on this side of his life:

"About his family Mandelstam almost never told me anything, and I did not inquire about them (the biographical interest in people . . . makes its appearance later in life). Only on one occasion—I do not remember in what connection—he gave me to understand that his relationship with his parents was not altogether satisfactory. He even exclaimed, 'It's terrible, terrible!' but since he was in general prone to overuse that expression, I immediately suspected him of exaggeration. And I still think that if Mandelstam's parents permitted him to live in Paris and occupy himself with whatever he wished they must not have been so indifferent to his wishes, and the family bonds did not lie so heavily upon him. In any case, he did not give one the feeling that he was constrained and bound. He was helpless in practical affairs, but spiritually he was independent and, I think, sufficiently confident in himself."

Our next glimpse of Mandelstam also reveals something of his relationship with his family. He turns up in the editorial office of *Apollon* accompanied by his mother, who apparently dragged the desperately embarrassed youth before the editor, Sergej Makovskij, for a showdown on his poetry. Years later, Makovskij, who emigrated to Paris, recalled the incident in a humorous memoir which makes the most of the dramatic contrasts involved: a sophisticated and erudite editor of one of the most elegant art journals of St. Petersburg, an awkward and mortified neophyte poet, and the loud and energetic wife of Emil' Mandelstam, leather merchant.[4] To Mme. Mandelstam's amazement, Makovskij praised some of the poems, and her son's career had its beginning in one of those almost Dostoevskian moments of scandal which were so often to mark his later life.

The early poems of Mandelstam, published in *Apollon*, earned him an immediate though an exceedingly narrow fame. They secured his entree into the literary circles of the capital and he quickly became an intimate in the cafés and salons where the life of the mind was then being lived, or at least celebrated.

In 1910 he went abroad for the second time, on this occasion to Heidelberg, where he studied Old French, and to Switzerland. Mandelstam's poems reveal such a seemingly firsthand knowledge of Italy that there has been a persistent attempt to discover whether he was actually there at least for a time, probably during this trip. The evidence, however, is only in the poetry, and even though this has been exhaustively catalogued by Gleb Struve, it is still inconclusive.[5] Those like Artur Lourié and others who knew Mandelstam closely at the time tell me that he was never in Italy.

[4] *Portrety sovremennikov* [Portraits of Contemporaries], (New York, 1955), pp. 377-379.

[5] "Ital'janskie obrazy i motivy v poézii Osipa Mandel'štama" [Italian Images and Motifs in the Poetry of Osip Mandel'štam], in *Studi in onore di Ettore Lo Gatto e Giovanni Maver* (Rome, 1962), pp. 601-614.

He returned to Russia to enter the University of St. Petersburg in the following year, after having crammed for the Greek entrance examination under the tutelage of the late Konstantin Mochul'skij.[6] Whether he finished the University is not definitely known, though it seems unlikely. The *Literaturnaja éntsiklopedija* (Literary Encyclopedia) states that he did, but the date is not given, and there is no other evidence of his having received a degree.

Study abroad and the first stages of literary success had greatly altered the character of the shy, easily embarrassed youth pictured in the earliest reminiscences of him. Karpovich saw Mandelstam again, for the last time, in 1912 and found his aspect far more imposing. "He had grown some side-whiskers à la Pushkin, and he already behaved himself like a *maître*."[7] It is worth recording, however, that Karpovich was speaking with Mandelstam on this occasion on the subject of poetry, a matter which he never treated lightly and in which he seldom deferred to the opinions of others. When his first book of poems, *Kamen'* (Stone), appeared in 1913 (at his own expense), his career was launched in earnest and his judgments more often solicited and given. There are numerous testimonies to Mandelstam's encounters with writers seeking his advice. When the poet Vsevolod Rozhdestvenskij's memoirs first appeared in the magazine *Zvezda* (Star) it was clear that the nameless poet whom he described as a kind of *arbiter elegantiarum* was Osip Mandelstam.[8] The physical description as well as the magisterial manner tallied with other accounts so well that it was impossible to mistake the identity of the young man who delivered himself so gravely and even sternly of decisive opinions in the matter of rhythm and imagery. But we need not rely on supposition alone, for when Rozhdestvenskij's memoirs, *Stranitsy zhizni* (Pages

[6] *Vstreča* [Meeting], 2 (1945), 30-31.
[7] Karpovič, *loc.cit.*   [8] 12 (1958), 116-135.

of Life), appeared in book form in 1962, Mandelstam's
name was permitted to appear (p. 129)—a hopeful sign.
These memoirs relate approximately to the time (1915)
when the well-known artist P. V. Miturich made a drawing of Mandelstam, depicting him, in the pose of Whistler's
mother, as a slender and rather haughty young man whom

one can well imagine as a member of the poetry jury
faced by Rozhdestvenskij. The writer Veniamin Kaverin
recalls a similar interview with Mandelstam some five
years later.[9] He had brought some of his poems—his best,
as he thought, because his most obscure—to Mandelstam
for the purpose of hearing his judgment. A similar interview with Viktor Shklovskij, the brilliant Formalist critic,

[9] "Kak ja ne stal poétom" [How I Did Not Become a Poet],
Oktjabr [October], 10 (1959), 131.

who had not even interrupted his exercise on a bicycle machine to deliver his ironic and withering comments, had just left Kaverin rather downcast. But, though Mandelstam was no more encouraging to the personal ambitions of Kaverin, there was something in his candid and passionate seriousness about poetry that proved almost consoling. "Mandelstam spoke severely, convincingly, with passion. There was no room here for irony. It was important to him that I cease writing poetry, and his words were a defense of poetry against me and those dozens and hundreds of young men and women who were busying themselves with the game of words. . . ."

For all his characteristic gaiety and wit, poetry was for Mandelstam anything but a game of words. Though this book deals only with his prose, perhaps it would be appropriate to interrupt the narrative of his life at this point in order to characterize (however lamely at this remove from the original language) the poetry upon which his fame chiefly rests.

· III ·

Mandelstam's career began at a time when literary taste was swinging, pendulum-like, away from the school of Symbolism which had dominated Russian poetry for some two decades. Symbolism, a term which covers some of the very best Russian poetry of the modern age, had brought with it in the 1890's a rejuvenation of poetic technique and an enormous refinement of poetic sensibility, but by the end of the first decade of this century its vitality had begun to wane and its inspiration to fade. The literary world, dominated exclusively by Symbolism for many years, saw the birth of several new "isms," each of them defined in large part by those features of Symbolism to which they were reacting negatively. Mandelstam's early poetry is written entirely in the spirit and manner of the Symbolists, the dominant masters of his formative years, but by the time the first collection of his poetry came out in 1913 he was already identifiable as one of the new group of Acmeists. The Acmeists, led at first by the gifted poet Nikolaj Gumilëv, were no less attentive to matters of form and technique than their predecessors. This concern for the craft of poetry is emphasized in the name *Tsekh poétov* (Guild of Poets) given to the loosely organized meetings held for the purpose of discussion, instruction, and mutual criticism. It was the mysticism of the Symbolists, their fascination with the occult and the other world, to which the Acmeists objected. They offered instead a poetry of this world, a celebration of the rose, as they said, for its own petals and perfume rather than for its supposed symbolic link to love in this world or the next. The Acmeists were far from rejecting the religious values of the Symbolists, but they refused to turn poetry into a church or themselves into hierophants. Gumilëv himself, whose personality is largely identical with the earliest form of Acmeism, was a man of distinctly masculine Christianity, and the world view of the Acmeists was declared to be manly, steady, and whole.

But if the Acmeists agreed in the demands to be made upon poetry, their answers to these demands were exceedingly various. Gumilëv's robust and colorful verse, filled with the exoticism of Africa and the clangor of all the wars of the West; Akhmatova's intimate, entirely feminine confessions; Mandelstam's recondite verbal elegance and the chaste architecture of his form—these were to be the leading representatives of the school.

Mandelstam's poetry also stands apart from that of his associates by virtue of its reputation for being extraordinarily difficult. As usual, much of the difficulty lies in the categorical expectations which readers bring to his work, but it is nevertheless true that he is not an easy poet. He is difficult in part because he refers to an immensely broad spectrum of culture and history as familiarly as a journalist might refer to the common news of the day. It may also be true that he is obscure to some because he requires of his reader, as Vladimir Pozner wrote, not only that culture which is acquired from books and museums but also that which is transmitted from father to son.[10]

For a modernist movement in verse, Acmeism was curiously conservative both in theme and technique. Mandelstam lived at a time when innovation in the prosodic ele-

ments of poetry was highly esteemed, but his rhymes and meters might, with few exceptions, seem familiar to the contemporaries of Pushkin. The diction of his slow, deliberately impeded lines occasionally recalled an even earlier

[10] *Panorama de la littérature russe contemporaine* (Paris, 1929), p. 265.

age, that of Derzhavin. But the imagery, the life's blood of his poetry, was wholly of his time, and of ours.

One of the most characteristic subjects of Mandelstam's poetic art is art itself. He wrote numerous poems which have their inspiration in other works of literature, and if the formula *l'art pour l'art* describes his manner, the matter of his verse, as Viktor Zhirmunskij has noted, deserves Schlegel's rubric *die Poesie der Poesie*.[11] A taste for Racine, rare in Russia, lies at the basis of his famous poem on the *Phèdre*, from which he also translated a portion. The "other world" of which he speaks here is not the "beyond" of the Symbolists but the world of arrested gesture and formal purity and balance which he saw in the classical art of Racine. The poems of Homer, the novels of Dickens, the Gothic tales of Edgar Poe—these are some of the other literary sources which furnish the impulse for numerous poems. It is so rare to find the art of architecture as a theme in Russian poetry that Mandelstam's attraction to it has been rather exaggerated. It is true, however, that some of his most successful lyrics are devoted to the great buildings of the world: the Hagia Sophia in Istanbul, the Cathedral of Notre Dame in Paris, the Admiralty in Petersburg, and the many churches of Moscow, the latter depicted in an exquisite poem as singers in a maidenly chorus. His poems on architecture are memorable also for his peculiar vision of buildings as organic structures, as processes of balance and tension, as a kind of joyous cooperative action to which each member contributes its share. This produces in the poem on Notre Dame, for example, a powerful tension between our sense of the cathedral as a massive, stationary structure and our sense of its continuous movement in the balancing of its parts. Through

[11] "Preodolevšie simvolizm" [Those Who Have Overcome Symbolism], *Russkaja Mysl'* [Russian Thought], 12 (1916). Reprinted in the same author's *Voprosy teorii literatury* [Problems of Literary Theory], (Leningrad, 1928).

all of Mandelstam's poems on architecture, on religious ritual, on the Greek epics and the poems of Ossian, and on historical subjects there runs a single unifying element—the element of grandness, of monumentality and solemnity. There is about much of his poetry a swelling sense of stateliness. The movement is often that of ritual, but if this ceremoniousness of tone is characteristic of him, it is also true that he could mock such gravity by describing a tennis match in a solemn and elevated style.

· IV ·

Mandelstam was not conscripted for the war, though it is unclear why he received the "white ticket" of exemption. Gumilëv enlisted at once, the Guild of Poets was disbanded, and the literary life of the capital was permanently altered. During some of the war years Mandelstam was in the south of Russia, mostly in the Crimea, where a large number of artists and writers had gathered. He found a haven in Koktebel', where Maksimilian Voloshin and his mother opened their dacha to many errant intellectuals, and also in Alushta at Aleksandr Aleksandrovich Smirnov's villa, which, together with several others nearby, bore the collective name *Professorskij ugolok* (Professors' Nook). The memoirs of Il'ja Ehrenburg and of Marina Tsvetaeva provide much of our knowledge of this Crimean retreat.[12] By the spring of 1918 Mandelstam was back in the north. His extraordinary adventure in Moscow with the terrorist Bljumkin (described below, p. 49f.) was the occasion for another hasty withdrawal to the Crimea His sojourn in Theodosia is described in the chapters under that name below. In 1920 he returned via Georgia to Petersburg, not

[12] Il'ja Ehrenburg, *Ljudi, gody, žizn'* [People, Years, Life], (Moscow, 1961), pp. 493-504; Marina Cvetaeva, "Istorija odnogo posvjaščenija" [The History of a Dedication], *Oxford Slavonic Papers*, xi (1964), 114-136.

without going through some of his usual misadventures. He was arrested by the military authorities on suspicion of being an enemy agent but was freed shortly thereafter. He tells this story in a brief magazine article called "The Mensheviks in Georgia."[13]

Post-war and post-revolutionary Petersburg, now Petrograd, was made habitable for intellectuals by the genius of Maksim Gorky, who was instrumental in having the former Eliseev mansion converted into a sanctuary for them. The House of the Arts, as it was called, figures largely in almost all the memoirs recalling those hungry and desolate years, but the most vivid evocation of the spirit of this extraordinary place is in Ol'ga Forsh's novella, *Sumasshedshij korabl'* (The Mad Ship), the title of which is itself an image of the house.[14] Mandelstam was one of the inmates. His reputation, formerly confined to a limited circle of intimates, was now much broader and more secure. *Stone* had appeared in a second edition in 1916, and the poems which he had brought back from the south were known to all the residents of the House of the Arts long before their publication in his second collection, *Tristia*, in 1922. He managed to support himself and his wife (he married Nadezhda Jakovlevna Khazina in 1922)[15]

[13] *Ogonëk* [Little Light], 20 (12 August 1923).

[14] Leningrad, 1931. This has recently been reprinted with a very useful introduction by Boris Filippov, Washington, D.C., 1964

[15] In all his writing Mandel'štam referred to his wife only once (in *Putešestvie v Armeniju* [Trip to Armenia]), and it was not until after the publication of his *Collected Works* in New York in 1955 that most of his friends, now émigrés in the West, even knew of his marriage. In disclosing the fact, Georgij Ivanov characteristically seasoned it with inventions of his own, such as that the marriage had been tragically unhappy and that a daughter, whose name he gave as Lipočka, had been born; see *Novyj Žurnal* [The New Review], XLIII (1955). Anna Axmatova, who knew Mandel'štam all his life, has now disclosed the falsity of these reports: there was never any daughter, and the Mandel'štams appear to have

by journalism, editorial work, and by translating for the publishing house *Vsemirnaja literatura* (Universal Literature), another of Gorky's enterprises. The summit of his career was the year 1928. In that year a collected edition of his poems appeared and so did all of the prose translated here (under the general title of *The Egyptian Stamp*). Soviet criticism of his work was still moderately mild, but the long night of the 1930's was already approaching. His last published work in the Soviet press was "A Trip to Armenia," which appeared in the magazine *Zvezda* in 1933. On 13 May 1934 at No. 3 Furmanov Street in Leningrad Mandelstam was arrested for having written the epigram on Stalin that we have described and that, in effect, was the end of his public existence.

Shortly after the arrest Mandelstam was actually brought before Stalin himself for a personal inquisition—in its own sinister way perhaps the profoundest tribute ever paid by the Soviet regime to the power of Mandelstam's pen. Stalin's personal concern in the matter is further attested in the following curious episode, which is here reported as it was received directly from Boris Pasternak:[16]

"One day Mandelstam's wife came to Pasternak to beg him to do what he could to get Osip out of jail. This was the first news he had had of Mandelstam's arrest; the two had never been close friends (even their stylistic evolution, as Pasternak once remarked, had proceeded in opposite directions: Mandelstam's from clarity towards obscurity, Pasternak's from complexity towards simplicity). However, Mandelstam's wife begged him to do what he could, and Pasternak promised to try to help. It happened about this

---

been a devoted couple. See her memoir in *Vozdušnye Puti* [Aerial Ways], IV (1965).

[16] "Impressions of Boris Pasternak," *The New Reasoner*, 4 (1958), 88-89. The author of this memoir, who wishes to retain the anonymity under which it was published, writes with an authority upon which readers can rely.

time that some high Government or Party dignitary died. In accordance with custom the body lay in state in the Columned Hall of the House of Unions, while Soviet notables stood guard of honor and the public filed past. Pasternak went to the Columned Hall to pay his last respects to the dead and noticed among the guard of honor someone he knew—I think it was Bukharin. He remembered Mandelstam's wife's request and stopped for a moment to ask Bukharin to see if he could do anything to help. Bukharin wasn't hopeful but said he would try. A few nights later a party was in progress in Pasternak's flat when the telephone rang. The voice at the far end asked if that was Comrade Pasternak; Comrade Stalin would like to speak to him from the Kremlin. A moment later a voice with a perceptible Georgian accent spoke: 'Is that Pasternak? This is Stalin.'

" 'Good evening, Comrade Stalin. By the way, this is not a leg-pull, is it?'

" 'No, no, this is Stalin, all right.'

"At the name of Stalin there was a hush in the room. Pasternak said, 'There are twenty-six people in the room and they're all listening. Does that make any difference?'

"Stalin said, 'No, that's all right. What's this about Mandelstam?'

" 'I'd like to do what I can to help him.'

" 'Do you think he's a very good poet?'

" 'You know, Comrade Stalin, you should no more ask one poet what he thinks of another than you should ask a pretty woman her opinion of another pretty woman's looks.'

" 'Then am I to take it you don't think much of him?'

" 'No, no, you've got me wrong. I'm a different sort of poet from him, that's all. I think he's a good writer.'

" 'Very well, thank you.' Pause. 'Why don't you ever come to see me?'

" 'I should have thought it was rather your place to invite me.'

"Stalin laughed and wished Pasternak a good evening and that was the end of the conversation. The next day Mandelstam was released. Pasternak had never heard from Stalin again."

But if Mandelstam was in fact released, as this account would have it, it was not for long. He was sentenced to three years of exile in Cherdyn', a small town near the upper reaches of the Kama and to the north of Solikamsk.[17] In Cherdyn' he attempted to kill himself by leaping from a hospital window, but the result was no more than a broken arm. At this point his wife's appeals to the Central Committee were answered to the extent that Mandelstam was permitted to choose another place of exile. The permission is said to have come from Stalin himself. Mandelstam chose Voronezh.

To exile a poet is one thing; to prevent him from writing poems is quite another. It is largely owing to these later poems (and to the dates and places of composition with which they are marked) that we can follow some of Mandelstam's progress in the next few years. He was sent to Voronezh, and the major fund of his poems, recently received in the West and published in 1965 under the editorship of Gleb Struve and Boris Filippov, is divided into the "First Voronezh Notebook" and the "Second Voronezh Notebook." In the first the earliest dated poem is marked "April 1935" and the latest "Winter 1936." The span of the second notebook is from "Winter 1936" to "May 1937." That he may have been in Voronezh long before the first

[17] Except for a few details, the following account of Mandel'štam's final years comes from information recently obtained by George Stuckow and published by him in *Survey*, 46 (January 1963), 151-155; *Mosty* [Bridges], 10 (1963), 150-159; *Russkaja Mysl'* [Russian Thought (Paris)], 5 February 1963; *Novoe Russkoe Slovo* [New Russian Word], 9 February 1963.

dated poem is hinted at by Ehrenburg, who writes, in the memoirs already cited, "I searched for him in Voronezh in the summer of 1934" (p. 496). This is, however, one of those maddening half-revelations for which Ehrenburg has a peculiar gift, so one cannot be sure.

In May 1937 the three years of Mandelstam's sentence expired and he and his wife returned to Moscow, where they lived temporarily in their former apartment. They were, however, not permitted the right of domicile in the capital and had to live in Kalinin, whence they went to Moscow from time to time. In the fall of 1937 they went to Leningrad, where they visited a number of old friends.

Almost exactly one year from the time of his release from Voronezh, Mandelstam was undergoing treatment at a sanatorium near Charust'e, a small station not far from Tarusa, when he was arrested again (1 May 1938). He was charged with counter-revolutionary activity (this was the height of the Great Purge) and sentenced to five years in one of the concentration camps of the Far East. The journey from Moscow to Vladivostok (5,391 miles) was made in the stage-by-stage fashion that is customary in the deportation of large bodies of prisoners. The state of Mandelstam's health at this time can be judged by observing the photograph of the aged man facing page 7, taken near the end of his life when he was only 45 years old; by recalling the frightful experiences of his exile; and by the fact that he was under institutional care at the moment of his arrest. The effect of this latest calamity was to drive him to and, for a time at least, over the brink of insanity. The following is quoted from the communication of an anonymous correspondent, translated and cited by George Stuckow:

"Suspecting that his guards had received orders from Moscow to poison him, he refused to eat any meals (they consisted of bread, herring, dehydrated cabbage soup, and sometimes a little millet). His fellow deportees caught him stealing their bread rations. He was subjected to cruel beating-up until it was realized that he was really insane. In the Vladivostok transit camp his insanity assumed a still more acute form. He still feared being poisoned and began again to steal food from his fellow inmates in the barracks, believing that their rations, unlike his, were not poisoned. Once again he was brutally beaten up. In the end he was thrown out of the barracks; he went to live near the refuse heap, feeding on garbage. Filthy, with long, gray hair and a long beard, dressed in tatters, with a mad look in his eyes, he became a veritable scarecrow of the camp. Occasionally, he was fed by the camp doctors, among whom there was one who had known him in Voronezh and admired his poetry."[18]

A later account by George Stuckow is based on more recent information than the above, which it somewhat corrects. It contains a letter written by Mandelstam from Vladivostok, probably during the latter part of October 1938, to his brother Aleksandr Emilievich (addressed as Shura and Shurochka) and his wife Nadezhda Jakovlevna (Naden'ka, Nadja). While the letter is naturally that of a distraught and terrified man, it is not the product of a deranged mind:

"Dear Shura!

"I am in Vladivostok, USVITL [apparently an abbreviated form of the camp name; the last three initials stand for 'corrective labor camp'], barracks 11. I got five years for counter-revolutionary activity, by decree of the OSO [an organ of the NKVD, the secret police]. By stages from Butyrki [prison] in Moscow on 9 September, arrived 12 October. Health very weak, totally exhausted, terribly thin, almost unrecognizable, but as for sending clothes, food, money—I don't know if there's any point. Try anyway. Terribly frozen without warm things.

[18] *Survey*, No. 46, p. 154.

"Dear Naden'ka, I don't know whether you're alive, my darling. Shura, you write to me right away about Nadja. This is a transit point. They didn't take me to Kolyma. May have to spend the winter.

"My dears, I kiss you.

Osja

"Shurochka, I'll write some more. We've gone out to work these last few days. That's raised my spirits. People are sent from this place, a transit camp, to the permanent camps. I apparently got 'sifted' and will have to get ready for the winter. And please, send me a radiogram and some money by wire."[19]

This is Mandelstam's last prose.

He was not to live through the winter of which he speaks with such apprehension, and death came to him on or about 27 December 1938. Il'ja Ehrenburg recalled Mandelstam with real warmth and, under the circumstances, considerable candor. Still, it is perhaps not to be wondered at that he should have averted his gaze from his friend's final agony, to which he lends a certain gentle, even "poetic," touch: "He was ill and had been sitting beside the fire reciting the sonnets of Petrarch."[20] There are other versions of a harder death.

· V ·

> *A* raznochinets *needs no memory—it is enough for him to tell of the books he has read, and his biography is done.*

The chapter on Vera Komissarzhevskaja in *The Noise of Time* begins in the following characteristically oblique way: "My desire is to speak not about myself but to track down the age, the noise and the germination of time. My memory is inimical to all that is personal." Was it in fact? Certainly this declaration is not without value to the stu-

[19] *NRS*, 9 February 1963.   [20] *Op.cit.*, p. 503.

dent of Mandelstam, but I doubt that its plain meaning can be accepted uncritically. On the one hand, there is that peculiar reticence about himself and his family that has so often been noted in the memoir literature about Mandelstam. And no reader of his autobiographical writings can remain unaware of the wholesale ellipsis which constitutes in large part the very aesthetic basis of his work. Those who are more familiar with his personal history will be sensitive to certain strange gaps, such as the failure even to mention the existence of his two brothers. Aunts, cousins, grandparents, and relatives too distant for reckoning throng his pages. We are afforded little vistas into the personal histories of governesses and workmen and shabby teachers of Hebrew, but of Aleksandr and Evgenij, with the first of whom, at least, he appears to have been quite close, there is not a syllable. In all of Mandelstam there is but one single reference to his wife, so obscure that the editors of his collected works claimed in a literary polemic never to have heard of her existence. His parents themselves are reduced to little more than their pronunciations. Certainly no one can imagine Mandelstam emulating the "Tolstoys and Aksakovs . . . with their epic domestic memoirs," which he professed to find incomprehensible.

And yet, what is one to do with the plain fact of the matter: that all of Mandelstam's prose is intensely and immediately personal when it is not openly autobiographical? It is so densely imbued with his Self that one tends soon to ignore this obvious and persistent element. It may be true that his autobiographical writings, like those of Gorky, are conspicuous for their continuous portraiture of other people, but those portraits are conveyed to the eye of the reader through the prismatic vision of a consciousness whose presence we constantly sense. Mandelstam is always there in his writing. This may be said even of his one known venture into what would at first appear to be fiction—*The Egyptian Stamp*. And his poetry, to which the word "impersonal" has so often been applied that it has become an unexamined critical cliché, requires only a closer and a more enlightened reading to be seen as the personal and intimate record that it is. He was preeminently the poet of the present moment, of the literal fact in all its particularity, believing that only the instant of the artist's perception has any chance of withstanding time's attrition, and it is just such poetry that is most closely linked to the actual personality and experience of the poet. It was, after all, the personal and immediate in his beloved Villon and even in Dante which Mandelstam regarded as the key to their permanence.

Mandelstam was possessed by the true taxonomical passion for sorting and arranging his impressions. It has been noted before that his people tend to be catalogued, and there is no more revealing example of this than the short "portrait gallery" of his classmates in the Tenishev School. Berkovskij spoke of this as Mandelstam's habit of returning all his little birds to their cultural nests.[21] But the same is true of all other phenomena in his artistic world. Objects, like people, have histories. They are the artifacts of a particular culture and derive from a specific time and place. Mandelstam may be conceived as a bemused stroller through his own personal waxworks, the museum of his past, where all the exhibits—from his mother's edition of Pushkin, through the brothers Krupenskij, "connoisseurs of wine and Jews," to that "Marxist propylaea," Karl Kautsky's Erfurt Program—are lovingly maintained behind glass. But the glass which separates him from what he describes serves also to reflect his own image and, in his perception, to superimpose himself over all that he sees. The author's denial of any interest in that phantasmal likeness of his own face is a curiosity which reveals one facet

[21] N. Berkovskij, *Tekuščaja literatura* [Current Literature], (Moscow, 1930), pp. 170-171.

of his psyche, but it will hardly dissuade the reader from observing that intense preoccupation with his own ego which is the very medium in which Mandelstam's prose exists.

The Russian title of *The Noise of Time* is *Shum vremeni*. Had the brief note of acknowledgment in the front of this book been really encyclopedic, it would have shown how abundantly I have availed myself of all the native Russian advice I could find in the task of turning Mandelstam into English, though this advice has not always been, as it could not be expected to be, in agreement. The translation of *shum* is difficult out of all proportion to the miniature size of this word. My first choice was "noise," and it found favor with some, but there was impressive insistence that *shum* is best rendered by "sound." On the point of yielding, I was stopped by that dean of scholiasts, Vladimir Nabokov, whose four-volume translation of and commentary on Pushkin's *Eugene Onegin* (New York, 1964) arrived in the nick of time. In his annotation of line 9 of One: xxxv—*Prosnulsja utra shum prijatnyj*, rendered by him as "Morn's pleasant hubbub has awoken"—Nabokov provides us with a characteristic little essay on the various nuances of *shum*. The transliteration in what follows is his:

"An analogous line occurs in *Poltava* (1828), pt. ii, l. 318: *razdálsya útra shúm igríviy*, 'morn's frisky hubbub has resounded.' Compare these epithets with those used by English poets, e.g., Milton's 'the busy hum of men' and John Dyer's 'the Noise of busy Man.'

"Generally speaking, the sense of *shum* implies a more sustained and uniform auditory effect than the English 'noise.' It is also a shade more remote and confused. It is at heart more of a swoosh than a racket. All its forms— *shum* (n.), *shumnïy* (adj.), *shumyashchiy* (part.), *shumet'* (v.)—are beautifully onomatopoeic, which 'noisy' and 'to noise' are not. *Shum* acquires a number of nuances in connection with various subjects: *shum goroda*, 'the hum of the city,' 'the tumult of the town'; *shum lesov,* 'the murmur of woods'; *shumyashchiy les,* 'the sough of forests'; *shumnïy ruchey,* 'the dinning stream'; *shumyashchee more,* 'the sounding sea,' the rote, the thud, and the roar of the surf on the shore—'the surgy murmurs of the lonely sea,' as Keats has it in *Endymion,* l. 121. *Shum* may also mean 'commotion,' 'clamor,' and so forth. The verb *shumet'* is poorly rendered by 'to be noisy,' 'to clatter.'" (Vol. 2, 143f.)

The solace which I find in this is not, of course, what Nabokov has to say about "noise," since he specifically rejects it in favor of "hubbub." It is the evidence of his uneasiness with the latter, which produces the delightful change-ringing on the various shades of *shum.* As in all such cases, the final choice is a matter of taste.

The relevance of these deliberations to Mandelstam's work is central. The insipid word "sound," which is virtually without overtones, cannot serve to describe the disjointed, elliptical style of these memoirs. If the faint but deliberate cacophony that arises from this jumbled juxtaposition of Finnish sleigh-bells, strolling brass bands, the alpine chill of concerts by Hofmann and Kubelik, the wheezing of Julij Matveich, and Vladimir Gippius's bellowing summons to the hack seems to the reader, as it does to me, inadequately reflected in "noise," let him contemplate in Nabokov's note some of the things to which Mandelstam's inner ear was attuned when he named his work *Shum vremeni.*

It is the type of autobiography that exposes the Self by showing its peculiar apperception of the people, the events, the large cultural and spiritual movements that have shaped it. It recalls that earlier masterpiece of evocative and reflective self-portraiture, Apollon Grigor'ev's *My Literary and Moral Wanderings,* now available to English readers in a new translation by Ralph Matlaw (New York, 1962).

Much of the following paragraph from that work will sound familiar to readers of Mandelstam:

"I intend to write a history of my impressions rather than an autobiography; I choose myself as an object, as a complete stranger, I look upon myself as a son of a particular era, and consequently only what generally characterizes the era ought to be included in my reminiscences: whatever concerns me personally will be included only insofar as it characterizes the era." (p. 11)

The memoirs of both are instinct with a sense of place, and there is even a partial similarity in the places themselves. Grigor'ev's locale was the district in Moscow on the left bank of the Moscow River called Zamoskvorech'e (literally: "beyond the Moscow"). It was in Grigor'ev's day a grimy quarter inhabited for the most part by the merchant class and notably lacking in the refinements of culture: a world made familiar in the dramas of Ostrovskij. The Jewish quarter of St. Petersburg, in the Kolomna district, had for Mandelstam much of the same significance. Baedeker's *Russia* (1914) notes this region of the city with a slightly averted gaze and offers no encouragement to the genteel traveller who might undertake a closer inspection, and in his story "The Portrait" Nikolaj Gogol depicts the Kolomna of the early nineteenth century in equally unflattering terms. The nostalgia inspired in both writers by the settings of their early lives is, like that of John Betjeman, onomastic and toponymic. Their pages, especially Mandelstam's, are saturated with names of streets, parks, shops, buildings and builders, writers and their works. For both, literature is the preserve most often pillaged for allusion and example. Grigor'ev can dispense with a description of his grandfather since Aksakov's description of *his* grandfather is available and presumed to be familiar to readers.

Mandelstam's constant immersion in literary culture makes it the very currency of his prose. One has a sense of reading a document written for a close circle of acquaintances, all of whom share an immense fund of cultural resource, available upon demand. To expend these monies in the furtherance of his intellectual commerce with his readers, Mandelstam had only to breathe a word or two, to sign the briefest of chits. It is, to be sure, his native Russian literature to which he, like Grigor'ev, most often alludes, but his range is broader and more European in scope. The commentary to this translation assumes much of this knowledge on the part of the new readers to whom it is addressed, for had all the writers and characters and titles of Russian literature been noted, it would have been far too long. What is more, I think that a good deal of the effect of Mandelstam's prose comes from our feeling of sharing with this civilized Russian such large areas of thought and response which can be summoned before our consciousness without being too much insisted upon. The Russian modernists who flourished around the turn of the century are still, in spite of many excellent translations and studies, not yet really familiar below the level of the cultural elite in the West. This is true even of the extraordinarily gifted painters, whose way has never been blocked by the barrier of language. An awareness of how little cultural translation we require beyond that of language—infinitely less than we need in the case of our own contemporaries in the Soviet Union!—can serve only to increase our pleasure and our understanding.

If the Russians gave us the great masters of realistic portraiture, Tolstoy and Dostoevsky, with their incredible ability to create whole families of living human presences, more vital and memorable than most of our actual acquaintances, it was they who also produced Nikolaj Gogol, that diabolically gifted puppet-master who causes his grotesque creatures to perform an endless *bouffonnerie* at the expense of the human race. Gogol's old friend, S. T.

Aksakov, passed a two-word judgment on *Dead Souls* which has remained one of the most illuminating things ever said of that book: he called it a *sborišče urodov* (an assembly of monsters). It is to this tradition that Mandelstam belongs, though one must immediately add that, for all his Gogolian tendency to caricature, he was infinitely more kindhearted. This may arise partly from the fact that virtually none of the characters in the pages of Mandelstam was wholly imagined, not even in the apparent fiction, and the kindliness of his literary portraiture is in keeping with the image we have of him in life. Even his epigrams, however witty they may be, contain little acid. He seldom wrote of people whom he disliked, and it is extraordinary to find any animus whatever in his pages unless it be aroused in the defense of poetry, the one subject on which he was unfailingly serious. Indifference to poetry, or ingratitude for it, or the callow assumption that any drivel might be "dragged into prominence" in its name—this was intolerable and could be dealt with unmercifully.

But the ordinary human creatures resurrected in his prose could hardly have complained of the queer guise in which they are brought before us, so gentle and loving is Mandelstam's humor.

Could Julij Matveich conceivably have objected to being portrayed as a sort of walrus wrapped in a beaver coat and with the improbably tender head of Bismarck on his shoulders? It seems most unlikely that these elements in his image could have outweighed the warmth and compassion which Mandelstam obviously feels for him. As in the case of the great fabulists, his pasquinades on the human race depend heavily on the equation of men with animals. The principal of the Tenishev School, Ostrogorskij, whose humor evidently delighted Mandelstam, was "a great scrofulous ape in a frock coat." Mandelstam is especially reminiscent of Gogol when he goes to the ultimate length of caricature: the reduction of a human portrait to one single feature. Thus Count Witte comes before us as a nose, and nothing more. The complex picture of Sergej Ivanych shows us the opposite extreme, for there are so many elements blended into the elaborate representation of him that one thinks rather of the technique of collage than of caricature. The controlling image is again that of an animal, this time the mythological chimera, a monster composed of the parts of various beasts, but if we dissect this monster we will find he consists of paper (he was an interlinear translation, he shed flimsy revolutionary tracts as he walked), of the police rock from which he had been chipped away, of cigarette smoke, and even of the delicious hot chocolate to which he was so passionately devoted. The face in this particular collage is composed of a crumpled student beret. Incidentally, would Beckett himself not envy the description of Sergej Ivanych's walk? "His walk resembled that of a man who had just been seized by the shoulder and led into the presence of some terrible satrap while trying to appear completely nonchalant."

Sergej Ivanych suffered a strange depletion of his revolutionary fervor after 1905 and went away to work in the Pulkovo Observatory. The chapter on him concludes: "If Sergej Ivanych had been transformed into a pure logarithm of stellar velocities or a function of space it would not have surprised me. He had to depart this world, such a chimera was he."

What is the technique here? It is essentially poetic—picturing one thing in terms of another. This device is so constant in Mandelstam that it becomes peculiarly his own, and one has almost a sensation of *déja lu* when one encounters in the Soviet writer Vera Inber this purely Mandelstamian sentence, recalling what was said of Sergej Ivanych: "From his constant and long-standing communion with the cosmos our teacher Foma Narcissovich had acquired a nebulosity of expression and the circular movements of the stars."[22]

Mandelstam's approach to characterization is one of extreme concentration by virtue of which a human figure is pictured in terms of the surroundings. The epithet applied to the voice of the Petersburg cabby is "oaty," which is an absurdity to readers who have not understood Mandelstam's surrealistic technique of displacing modifiers on the principle of proximity. The horse of the cabby is not otherwise summoned into existence than by this single qualifier of his master's voice.[23] Mandelstam's relative, the literary historian Vengerov, is revealed to us smirking into his "dense *ant* beard." But the adjective for the word "ant" does not really characterize the beard itself so much as it does Vengerov's monumental tolerance for drudgery and his regular itinerary from apartment to card catalogue and back. The synagogue in the Kolomna District is characterized by the word "leonine," but that hardly describes the building itself, which was earlier compared to an "elegant exotic fig tree." Its presence in this sentence is to be accounted for by the near proximity of the name Samson: "The Cantor, like Samson, collapsed the leonine building. . . ." The entire building has been infected by the associations hovering about the name of Samson. There is a blending of the central object of vision with the qualities of the periphery, which, however, yields not a blur but a heightened intensity of awareness. In Mandelstam a man's occupation and preoccupation are all-important, for in this fictive world a man becomes, literally, what he does.

[22] "Smert' Luny" [The Death of Luna], trans. by Walter Morison in Richard Newnham (ed.), *Soviet Short Stories* (Baltimore, 1963), p. 17.
[23] Cf. Berkovskij, p. 173f.

· VI ·

"It is terrifying to think that our life is a tale without a
plot or a hero, made up out of desolation and glass, out
of the feverish babble of constant digressions, out of the
delirium of the Petersburg influenza."

This sentence occurs toward the end of *The Egyptian
Stamp*, the single example of Mandelstam's narrative prose
and one of the few examples of surrealist fiction to be found
in all of Russian literature. We might take these words as a
clue to the pattern of the tale itself, which is composed in a
kind of delirious key and consists of just such a feverish
babble of constant digressions. In Mandelstam's serious
writing it is the nearest approach to dealing directly with
the bleak reality of his time and place, though it can
seem, in the flaunting of its various opacities, to be as remote from that reality as poems like "Nashedshij podkovu"
(The Finder of a Horseshoe) or the terrible "Grifel'naja
oda" (The Slate Ode). It represents that reality in a frag-
mented, multifaceted manner which strives for an artistic
equivalency to the fractured life of the period. The desolation and glass are those of Petersburg—temporarily Petrograd, though never recognized as such by Mandelstam—
during the "Kerenskij Summer" between the two revolutions of 1917.

Perhaps there were other reasons, too, for the elliptical
manner. The central character strikes one almost at once
as a familiar figure: here is one of the legion of "little
men," the spineless or hapless but in any case heroically
weak victims of Russian literature. We know him. But as
we read, our familiarity with him seems to grow and to
become more specific, our sense of his significance deepens,
and we are at the end finally aware that this late descendant
of Akakij Akakievich represents in the context of his time
a statement which in a more naked form, shorn of the

ambiguity of its many levels, might have been not only less poetic but certainly less prudent.

In noting that all of the prose translated here is personal and autobiographical, we must stress that the "fictional" *Egyptian Stamp* is no exception. To the best of our present knowledge, it is as close as Mandelstam ever came to creating a conventional plot, a purely imagined story, and it is my contention that even here he did not come so close as it may seem. For all the prismatic surrealism through which we see the background of the novella, it is still vividly the actual stone and glass of Petersburg. The same may be said of certain of the characters: they derive with hardly a change of name from actual acquaintances of Mandelstam. And it seems to me that the central event itself recapitulates, this time with considerably more disguise, an episode from Mandelstam's personal history.

His beloved Petersburg—the classical and eighteenth-century nature of which he caressed in his poetry with the Derzhavinian name "Petropol'"—has become animal: "loathsome as if it were eating a soup of crushed flies." Everything has gone to pieces, like the style of narration. Violence and lawlessness are unrestrained, since the government, "sleeping like a carp," has vanished. It is a background against which the impotence and futility of the dreamy little hero with the queer name of Parnok impress us all the more. But Parnok has the artist's antidote against horror—a retreat into his abstracted interior musing, the description of which vies with the external narration as the focus of the novella. There is in general an uneasy balance between the real and the imagined: Parnok's strabismal vision is forever half on one, half on the other. His inner thoughts are nostalgic, poetic, culture-laden; they sometimes descend into a fatigue-induced playing with words that have snagged his attention.

Parnok loves music, and his presence alone in the foreground of the narration is sufficient to scatter musical images throughout the description of his surroundings. Another example of that saturation technique which we have already discussed is Parnok's entry into the Polish laundry, transforming it into a kind of Renaissance concert.

The narrative covers one day in the hero's life. There are two plot lines, both quite uncomplicated except in the manner of their telling, and there is no visible connection between them on the level of straight narration. In one, the frame of the novella, Parnok spends his day in the unsuccessful attempt to retrieve certain items of his clothing which seem to gravitate mysteriously into the hands of a certain Captain Krzyżanowski of the Horse Guards. In the second he tries vainly to prevent the mob murder of some unfortunate little man, like himself, who is accused of having stolen a silver watch.

Parnok's day, like Bloomsday, consists essentially of a journey through the city. He goes first to the tailor Mervis in a vain attempt to recover a morning coat, stealthily repossessed during the night for lack of payment. He is next briefly discovered in the chair of a barber who is rather more like an executioner than a barber. He then encounters an acquaintance, Father Nikolaj Aleksandrovich Bruni, and goes with him to a Polish laundry, where he tries, again vainly, to retrieve some shirts. The laundry is Dantesque, an ominous tableau from Mandelstam's Inferno, where hot clouds of suffocating steam half reveal six twittering girls spraying water from their mouths onto the clothes to be ironed. When Parnok spies his shirts, the girls tell him that they belong to Captain Krzyżanowski, the first mention of that gray eminence whose presence is to be felt thenceforward in the story and who is finally to usurp even Parnok's place in it. Parnok turns up next in a dentist's chair, where he is having a tooth filled (things are forever being done *to* Parnok). It is from this vantage point that our hero hears a lynch mob outside in Gorokhovaja Street. Parnok—the little man par excellence, the rabbit-blooded Parnok—races out on a desperately quixotic adventure: to save the life of the nameless, faceless little man who is being taken to the Fontanka, where he will be drowned for some crime that is never specified. Parnok's mission has all the attributes of a nightmare. He must attract attention, that of the authorities, in order to stop the murder, and yet not attract the attention of the mob to himself. Nothing helps. The law has vanished. Parnok's single encounter with Captain Krzyżanowski takes place, but the military officer, elegant and masterful in his uniform and with a lady on his arm, answers Parnok's pleas for help with a cool banality and vanishes into a café. The murder, we are to assume, takes place.

This is the midpoint of the story. All Parnok's important failures have taken place, and there is really nothing more for him to do. His external adventures are henceforth far less clearly described. The narrative dissolves into a series of evocative and shifting pictures, the function of which is extremely complex: to suggest the spiritual condition of Parnok by the musings and memories that shut actuality out of his mind and at the same time to reveal by a few hints some of the further events of the day. These episodes succeed each other in a curious mosaic pattern, the intrinsic charm of which seduces the attention from any direct concern with the events of the original narrative, which one feels to be taking its ordinary course just beyond or behind the language before us. This language has the qualities of Mandelstam's best poetry: condensation, form, grace, observation, wit. Were that its only reason for being, it would be sufficient, and the style in large measure *becomes* the plot of this *commedia erudita*. The foreground is momentarily occupied by a procession of deaf-mutes whose gesture-language is pictured as a literal weaving of the fabric of the air (Mandelstam had a singular fondness for textile images). They make their way across the vast Palace Square—the immense perspectives of Petersburg make it God's own setting for surrealism—and this tableau fades to an extraordinary passage in which the visual aspect of the musical notation of various composers is impressionistically brought to life. The illusion of third-person narrative is suddenly shattered by the author's own voice, which breaks in to cry, "Lord! Do not make me like Parnok! Give me the strength to distinguish myself from him." And so the novella proceeds: anecdotal family memoirs; here and there a glimpse of the characters and situations with which we started; orgies of metaphor, transmogrifying the objects of Parnok's vision and memory; the death of an Italian soprano accompanied by fire alarms which her expiring fancy transmutes into the overture of her London debut.

The rest of the objective narrative is this. Krzyżanowski and his lady go to a performance of *Giselle* at the Mariinskij. On the way there Krzyżanowski somehow confuses Parnok with the victim of the lynch mob—an instructive error. Later the tailor Mervis is discovered hurrying through the street on an errand: to take Parnok's coat to (of course) Captain Krzyżanowski. There is one last picture of Parnok. It is the evening of the day covered by the narrative, but he does not return home (he is, anyway, homeless). Instead, he occupies his worthless time with futile dreams of getting a position as a translator in the Foreign Ministry. It is his base genealogy that will prevent his being accepted there. Meanwhile, it is Captain Krzyżanowski, his luggage packed with Parnok's coat and best shirts, who is to escape from the hallucination of Petersburg. He takes the express to Moscow, where he stops at the elegant Hotel Select.

If this account errs, it errs perhaps in imparting greater clarity and even obviousness to the story than is actually there on a first reading. But it will surprise no one to learn that the story itself, the primary surface narrative, hardly matters. It is no more the focus here than some of the equally trivial plots of Gogol are his focus.

The surface events of Parnok's day are indeed the surface, and below them one can discern at least two more levels: that of the literary tradition and that of autobiography. The former is the more important, and I deal with it first.

In a way, to be sure, any work that participates importantly in a specific heritage, a distinct one, may be said to contain by virtue of our examining it from that point of view the level of the "tradition." That is not what is intended here. *The Egyptian Stamp* not only forms a part of, while significantly extending, one of the most viable and important themes of the Russian literary tradition, but it also uses specific earlier manifestations of that theme for the purpose of making its unique declaration. The chief among its sources is Dostoevsky's weird tale *Dvojnik* (The Double). But since it is generally acknowledged that Dostoevsky's tale is very much in the debt of an even weirder tale, Gogol's *Nos* (The Nose), then clearly Mandelstam's work depends not only on *The Double* but also on *The Nose*.

Dostoevsky's early apprenticeship to his master Gogol is well known. *Bednye ljudi* (Poor Folk), which made Dostoevsky's fame in 1846, is so clearly an answer to Gogol's *Shinel'* (The Overcoat) that he even goes to the length of having his characters read and comment upon the earlier work. The importance of *The Nose* for *The Double* is, however, not made so patently evident. It lies rather in the fact that Dostoevsky reproduced in broad outline the essential framework of the plot: the split in identity of the central character. His Mr. Goljadkin is, like Gogol's Kovalëv, a civil servant hounded by real and imagined enemies who prevent his getting on in the struggle up the ladder of civil service ranks. Mr. Goljadkin, unlike Kovalëv, is clearly mad, a fact which he himself suspects from the outset, and he becomes more so in the course of the narrative until, in the final scene, he is being driven off to the lunatic asylum as his double bounds along beside the carriage with expressions of feigned solicitude. This double, this antagonistic other self, is Dostoevsky's equivalent for Kovalëv's fantastic nose, which detaches itself mysteriously (perhaps cut off by the barber, but perhaps not) and takes up its independent existence in a civil service rank higher than that of Collegiate Assessor Kovalëv himself. Like the nose, the second Mr. Goljadkin is as great a success in the constant internecine war of the civil service as the first Mr. Goljadkin is a failure. He shines at just those enterprises at which his original would most like to shine: he is, in fact, as much the projection of Mr. Goljadkin's inner self as the nose was an actual part of Kovalëv's outer self. And in both cases it is the self as its own worst enemy. In addition to all this, which amounts to nothing less than that "serious idea"—the antagonism of the self—to which Dostoevsky was later to ascribe such central importance, there are little touches betraying his preoccupation with Gogol's earlier treatment of the theme: Goljadkin, repeating the identical actions of Kovalëv, arises from sleep at the beginning of the narrative and fusses about before a mirror, anxious lest a pimple might have appeared on his face overnight.

The Nose and *The Double* represent merely one pair of closely linked mutations of the theme. The little wretched self-divided hero has of course many incarnations in the history of Russian literature, beginning, it has been suggested, as far back as the hapless youth in the seventeenth-century *Tale of Gore Zlochast'e*.[24] Mandelstam's hero Parnok belongs in this line, but his closest relative is the one nearest to our modern sensibility: Mr. Goljadkin. And the progenitor of both is Gogol's *The Nose*.

For all its vastly more complex and sometimes baffling

[24] William E. Harkins, "The Pathetic Hero in Russian Seventeenth-Century Literature," *American Slavic and East European Review*, 4 (1955), 512-527.

structure and symbolism, *The Egyptian Stamp* presents the identical basic situation that we find in the works of Gogol and Dostoevsky: the hero, a helpless little man, finds his own identity split in two, the second half being endowed with all those attributes of power and invulnerable knowledge of the world lacking in the first. And the double uses his superiority to antagonize and persecute the hero. To put it briefly, Parnok is to Captain Krzyżanowski as Kovalëv is to the Nose and as Mr. Goljadkin the Elder is to Mr. Goljadkin the Younger. Mandelstam, like Dostoevsky in *Poor Folk*, makes his intention unmistakably clear to the reader by actually mentioning the hero of his model, and, moreover, by including that hero precisely in the list of Parnok's *ancestors*:

"Yes, with such relatives one could not go far. But—wait a moment—how is that not a pedigree? How not? It is. What about Captain Goljadkin? And the collegiate assessors, to whom 'the Lord God might add intelligence and money'? All those people who were shown down the stairs, publicly disgraced, insulted in the forties and fifties of the last century, all those mutterers, windbags in capes, with gloves that had been laundered to shreds, all those who do not 'live' but 'reside' on Sadovaja and Podjacheskaja in houses made of stale sections of petrified chocolate and grumble to themselves: 'How is that possible? Not a penny to my name, and me with a university education?'"

It is interesting to note that in the original version of this passage the name Goljadkin appeared without any military rank. Both Mr. Goljadkin and his Double held the rank of Titular Councilor, the ninth of the fourteen civil service grades, equivalent to the military rank of Captain of Infantry (*kapitan*) or Captain of Cavalry (*rotmistr*). Krzyżanowski is a Captain of Cavalry, and when Mandelstam republished the novella in book form he added the word "Captain" before Goljadkin's name (it is not there in Dostoevsky), thus clearly reinforcing the desired association.

But Parnok recalls Mr. Goljadkin in other ways, in his habits and even in certain verbal responses. Mr. Goljadkin, waiting for two hours on the cold landing of the back stairs in a torment of indecision before breaking uninvited into the ballroom, comforts himself with little, random, irrelevant thoughts:

"Having just quoted, as has already been said, the very pertinent phrase of the former French minister, Villèle, Mr. Goljadkin, for what reason is not known, immediately recalled the former Turkish vizier Martsimiris, as well as the beautiful Margravine Luise, about both of whom he had also read at some time or other in a book."[25]

After entering the brilliant company at the dance being given by his superior, Mr. Goljadkin, immediately conspicuous, is racked by self-consciousness and embarrassment. As Parnok was later to do, he retreats into inconsequence, into a purely verbal innocence and innocuousness:

" 'That gentleman is wearing a wig,' thought Mr. Goljadkin, 'and if he were to take it off, his head would be just exactly as naked as the palm of my hand.' "[26]

This prefigures the identical habit of Parnok. Racing down the stairs into the street where the lynch mob is carrying its victim to the Fontanka, he soothes his terror with just such an irrelevancy: "Buttons are made of animal blood!" Earlier Parnok had "managed to think" of the mob: "All these people are brush salesmen."

Goljadkin moves by short, quick steps—the gait of Parnok, as is often noted. The central event in Goljadkin's wretched little history is his ignominious expulsion from the ball, and it is just such expulsion, again translated into the surrealistic idiom, that is the fate predicted for Parnok:

[25] F. M. Dostoevskij, *Sobranie sočinenij* [Collected Works], (Moscow, 1956), I, 240.
[26] *Ibid.*, p. 245.

"They will throw you out one of these days, Parnok, throw you out with frightful scandal and shame . . . they'll take you by the arm and pf-t-t! . . . out of the Symphony Hall, out of the Society of Friends and Amateurs of the Last Word, out of the Circle for Grasshopper Music, out of the salon of Mme. Bookbinder . . . who knows where else? . . . but out you will go, disgraced, vilified. . . ."

Parnok and Krzyżanowski fall easily into the paradigm prescribed by their earlier shapes in the tradition. Parnok's dream is to get a position in government service, but Captain Krzyżanowski, as the proprietress of the laundry relates, is not only a success in the service of the government but even a hero. Parnok was attracted to women after his fashion, but on sensing their distress in his presence retreated into "wild, bombastic, twittery language." Krzyżanowski, on the other hand, has a lady whose "criminal, pink little ear" is receptive to "the sweet nothings of the Horse Guard." Parnok's pitifully limited aim during the day in which we follow his activities is to recover his coat and shirts, but it is Krzyżanowski who, without even trying or seeming to care, gets possession of them and carries them off to Moscow.

It is clear that certain of Mandelstam's secondary characters are also drawn from the two sources dealt with here. What is the barber in *The Egyptian Stamp* but a descendant of the barber in *The Nose*? His lavatory is a chopping block, and he is presented as an executioner, a characterization that can be accounted for (given the correspondences already pointed out) only by his being modeled after Gogol's Ivan Jakovlevich, whose shop sign advertised his surgical services and who was, indeed, suspected of having cut off Kovalëv's nose. The presence of the dentist is also probably to be explained by the doctor in each of the earlier works, though the question of why it was precisely a dentist who was chosen is perhaps to be explained by

Mandelstam's own pathological dread of dentists, of which more later.

But there is more to the lineage of Parnok and his story. If the parallels with *The Nose* and *The Double* account for some elements of the story (they would appear to account almost entirely for Krzyżanowski), they leave others unexplained. I do not expect to discover some earlier incarnation in Russian literature for each personage in Mandelstam's tale, but, still, the tailor Mervis plays a central enough part to invite some speculation. Who is he?

Among the works offered as belonging more or less significantly to the general background of *The Egyptian Stamp,* Berkovskij mentions Pushkin's *Mednyj vsadnik* (The Bronze Horseman), Gogol's *Zapiski sumasshedshego* (Notes of a Madman), and Dostoevsky's *The Double.* In a brief prefatory note to their French translation of the novella, D. S. Mirsky and Georges Limbour mention Dostoevsky's *Idiot* and Tolstoy's *Anna Karenina* as well as *The Double.* Viktor Shklovskij mentions *The Bronze Horseman* and *The Double.*[27] It is remarkable that these lists draw our attention to certain liaisons which, while genuine, are far more tenuous than those with a work which they neglect to mention: Gogol's *Shinel'* (The Overcoat). After *The Double,* this is surely the most important literary source of Mandelstam's tale. For one thing, it answers the above question about Mervis.

The parallel with *The Overcoat* is striking indeed. It is enough to point out that Gogol's story is about Akakij Akakievich Bashmachkin, a kind of archetype of the civil servant—desperately poor, terrified of his superiors, the butt of his fellows—whose entire being is concentrated toward one end, the possession of an overcoat; that he is at the

[27] Berkovskij, p. 177; the translation by Mirsky and Limbour, "Le timbre égyptien," appeared in *Commerce,* xxiv (1930), 119-168; Šklovskij, "Put' k setke" [Way to the Net], *Literaturnyj kritik* [Literary Critic], 5 (1933), 115.

mercy of a malign tailor named Petrovich; and that he is finally robbed of his precious coat to realize how important are the links between it and *The Egyptian Stamp*. Mandelstam's central plot is, after all, about a little man striving without success to get back a coat of which he has been robbed. There is something about that coat itself that recalls Gogol's story: it is a *vizitka*, a morning coat or cutaway, which we may imagine as rather out of place in the grim milieu of this story, and which, moreover, is above Parnok's station in life. So was the overcoat of Akakij Akakievich too grand for him. It may be that for Dostoevsky, attacking Gogol's conception, the overcoat was a contemptible, unworthy object of human desires; but for Akakij himself, we must remember, it was almost too lofty an object for his aspirations.

The coat is functional in another way. It provides an organic link between the two principal streams of the tradition to which Mandelstam is adding a modern instance. I take Pushkin's Evgenij in *The Bronze Horseman* and Akakij Akakievich as typical of one stream: the little loser overwhelmed by large, exterior, objective forces— the very elements themselves, the consequences of the Petrine transformation, the inhumanity of the social structure. Kovalëv and Goljadkin represent the other stream: the antagonists are their other selves, parts of their divided personalities. This neat dichotomy must not be made to bear more than it can bear; if we look closely we see that there are elements of the first in the second and vice versa. To define the hero-victims by their antagonists is not to say the last word about them. But essentially it holds that we are dealing with undivided as against divided central characters, and the coat serves to unify this tradition in Mandelstam's novella. The goal of Parnok's desire is that of Akakij's, and it is carried off in the suitcase of his antagonistic double.

Parnok bears the greatest resemblance, as I have indicated, to Mr. Goljadkin; but there is at least one feature that reminds us of Akakij Akakievich: "At the beck and call of my consciousness are two or three little words: 'and there,' 'already,' 'suddenly.'" This recalls the unfortunate Akakij's almost unintelligible speech, consisting for the most part of prepositions, adverbs, and entirely meaningless particles.

Mervis, then, the tailor of Parnok's too-grand coat, is the direct spiritual descendant of Gogol's Petrovich. And he even bears a certain physical resemblance. The latter was blind in one eye and his face was disfigured by pockmarks. Of his tailor Mandelstam writes: "I must confess that I love Mervis—I love his blind face, furrowed by wrinkles that see." Petrovich's shrewish wife is not represented by Mervis' wife, who congratulates her husband on his cleverness in stealing back Parnok's coat, but her characteristics, like the characteristics of her smoke-filled kitchen, would seem to have been transferred to the furious proprietress of the laundry and her steamy shop, where Parnok also goes in his futile search for his clothes.

If Mandelstam's story is an ingenious combination of numerous elements from earlier works, the question why he did it may prove interesting. Are we to suppose him so poor in invention that he was compelled, in his only attempt at contriving an objective narrative, to borrow characters and situations from his predecessors? I do not think anyone even slightly acquainted with Mandelstam's work could accept that explanation. He had in fact an astonishingly inventive mind. One's feeling in reading him is constant and unflagging amazement—amazement precisely at the novelty and originality of his vision, and the uniquely personal character of his conception of the world, so personal that his individual imprint on whatever he created is immediately recognizable as "Mandelstamian." There can be no argument with Berkovskij's remark about his "lofty arrogance" in approaching the world of objects as the "last name-giver."[28] For the answer we must look rather to the complexity of Mandelstam's vision. Audacity of purpose, not paucity of invention, led him to utilize for his own special aims Gogol's and Dostoevsky's themes and characters. In order fully to grasp this complexity and audacity, it will be necessary to turn to the third of the principal levels of *The Egyptian Stamp*: the elliptical and elusive references to Mandelstam's own life.

One must deal here with allusion, often cryptic enough, with "tone," and with scattered, fractional details which, taken separately, could scarcely be regarded as conclusive, but together impress one with the extent to which Mandelstam was writing of himself. We know little of his life, as I have said, but it is clear that we know quite enough to see that a good deal of it has found its way into the ostensible fiction which we are considering.

There are two sorts of autobiographical reference in *The Egyptian Stamp*. The first is thoroughly private and consists of occasional references to and verbal echoes from his own work, especially from *The Noise of Time*, and also of some of the personal characteristics of Mandelstam which we find abundantly in the memoir literature devoted to him. An example of this kind of reference is to be seen in the last episode of Chapter VI. Captain Krzyżanowski and his companion are strolling along Ofitserskaja, where they drop into Aboling's lamp store, but we are told that "they never stopped by Ejlers' flower shop." Why do we require this bit of negative information? In the chapter entitled "Finland" in *The Noise of Time* Mandelstam mentions his family's constant move from apartment to apartment. One of their apartments was located on Ofitserskaja above that same Ejlers' flower shop. Is this autobiographical? I think that it is. Mandelstam, as this novella and his poetry show, had an acutely developed sense of place. A predominant mood in his work is that of

[28] Berkovskij, p. 160.

nostalgia, an elegiac sense of the past, and Mandelstam's nostalgia, as we have noted, was heavily dependent upon the actual names of places and things in Petersburg. There were a number of flower shops bearing the name of Ejlers in Petersburg, for they belonged to one chain, but there was only one on Ofitserskaja, and it was over that one that the Mandelstams lived. It had for him a purely domestic and personal connotation, like a family joke which means nothing to an outsider. The grandmother of Giselle is said to be pouring out milk, "probably almond." This is doubtless a verbal echo of the passage in *The Noise of Time* about his own grandmother and the "bitter, almond taste" of the dainties which she was forever offering. The scalpers behind the Mariinskij Theater, which was on the edge of the Jewish quarter in Petersburg, have their predecessors in the earlier work.

Whence the Polish laundry so vividly described by Mandelstam? The laundries of Petersburg were not traditionally or stereotypically operated by Poles as they are supposed to be by Chinese in the United States. We find the source in a passage from the memoirs of Mandelstam's friend, the cubo-futurist Benedikt Livshitz:

"By the way, it was none other than Mandelstam who disclosed to me the mysteries of 'savoir vivre' in Petersburg, beginning with the secret of how to obtain credit at the Stray Dog cabaret and ending with the Polish laundry where one could, by paying triple the regular price, get a shirt beautifully washed and stiffly starched in an hour's time —a really invaluable convenience in view of the meagreness of our wardrobes."[29]

It should be noted that this identifies not only the Polish laundry but even the practice of labeling one's wash "urgent," a habit which the outraged proprietress mentions in her general indictment of Parnok.

[29] *Polutoraglazyj strelec* [The One-and-a-Half-Eyed Archer], (Leningrad, 1933), p. 264.

Not only the Polish laundry, but one of the central figures in the scene at the laundry—Father Nikolaj Aleksandrovich Bruni—is also drawn from the personal life of the author. This is the actual name of a priest who was a close friend of Mandelstam. He was the brother of the artist Lev Bruni, who painted a portrait of Mandelstam, and a member of the prominent family which included the more famous artist Fëdor Antonovich Bruni (1799-1875), known for his immense academic canvasses on biblical and historical subjects. A member of the Academy and at one time director of the Academy of Fine Arts, F. A. Bruni was the son of an Italian painter who immigrated to Russia. He was celebrated for his decorations in St. Isaac's Cathedral in Petersburg. It was undoubtedly this long family association with painting which suggested to Mandelstam the conclusion of the scene in the laundry: "All this cries out to be painted on a ceiling."[30]

What is perhaps still more surprising is that the central character himself, Parnok, actually existed. His real name was Valentin Jakovlevich Parnakh, and the slight change in names is to be explained as follows. Parnakh, a Jew, was the brother of the minor poetess and critic Sofija Parnakh who wrote under the nom de plume of Andrej Poljanin and who legally changed her surname, perhaps in order to escape the disadvantages of its conspicuously Jewish sound, to Parnok, a name which is neither Jewish nor Russian, but merely strange. Parnakh left Russia and lived for a long time in Paris, where he published several books of his poetry in the early 1920's. His principal concern as a writer, however, was the dance; he published a brief history of the dance and wrote widely for dance periodicals. In Paris he spelled his name both "Parnakh" and "Parnac." It is altogether possible that Mandelstam was under the im-

---

[30] For the identification of Father Bruni I am indebted to Artur Lourié, who has kindly shared with me many memories of his friend Mandel'štam.

pression that he had, like his sister, changed his name; but it is also possible that he simply preferred the new name for its strange quality, for its queer appropriateness to the literary character. The Parnok of the story seems, though, to have been drawn rather literally from his model. Small of stature, slight of build, he is described by those who knew him as a nervous, restless little eccentric whose salient feature seems to have been his conspicuously sharp, shiny little shoes—the little "sheep hooves" so often ascribed to the fictional Parnok.[31] Picasso's portrait of him—luckily representational—shows a narrow-shouldered man with a rather large head, thrown back, as it chances, exactly in the haughty gesture which all memoirists of Mandelstam recall in their subject. There is, in fact, a striking resemblance between the portraits of Mandelstam by Miturich and Bruni and the portrait of Parnakh by Picasso.

Parnok would seem to be complicated enough, what with his complex literary genealogy and now his real-life source, but we have not yet come to the end. For Parnok was, finally, Mandelstam. This might suggest itself soon enough to anyone familiar with the reminiscences devoted to Mandelstam, where he is pictured in ways that make not only his physical but even his spiritual similarity to Parnok unmistakable. He was also small and rather frail. Nearly everyone who wrote of his appearance seems to have been struck by one aspect of it: he reminded most people of a bird. In fact, he seems to have reminded himself of a bird, for that is the way he pictures himself in the chapter from *Theodosia* called "The Old Woman's Bird." He walked with an eccentric, bouncy little step. He was pain-

[31] For my knowledge of the real-life source of Parnok I am indebted first of all to a Soviet writer who requests anonymity. I must assure the reader that his authority is beyond question. For linking the brother of the poetess Parnok to the Parnax of Paris, and for other information about him, I am obliged to my colleague Nina Berberova.

fully shy, excessively prone to take offense, terrified of unboiled water, and suffered from such an inordinate fear of dentists that he preferred to let his teeth rot in his head rather than submit to treatment. (Hence, I presume, the transformation of the doctor of his models into a dentist, and also the acidly sardonic treatment of him—"I love dentists for their wide horizons. . . .")[32]

In dealing with the literary sources of this tale, I have, it will be observed, treated only one of the two plot lines, that of the lost clothes. There is nothing in the other works that will account for the central episode: Parnok's paradoxical heroism in trying to save a nameless, faceless victim from the fury of a lynch mob. For this, we must go to Mandelstam's own life.

The principal authority for the *details* of the following story is, I must warn the reader, Georgij Ivanov, whose writings about Mandelstam contain a remarkable amount of fancy along with fact (as I shall undertake to show in a later study).[33] But the anonymous informant to whom I referred above has assured me of the basic veracity of this particular story, and of other stories which tend to lend this one plausibility.

Shortly after the Revolution, Mandelstam—so Ivanov's story goes—was at a drinking bout attended by both Bolsheviks and Left Socialist Revolutionaries during the period of their collaboration. Mandelstam was there because it was a place where sweets, his nearly pathological appetite for which is well documented, could be obtained. One of the most prominent of the Left SR's, Bljumkin,

---

[32] The word *dantist* (dentist)—and also *farmacevt* (druggist)—could have additional meanings, undoubtedly of importance here. Poets and artists used them for literary hangers-on, "squares" or "tourists" who frequented the cafes as mere spectators; but since a great many dentists and druggists in St. Petersburg were Jews, the words are faintly anti-Semitic in connotation, suggesting specifically Jewish "squares."

[33] Georgij Ivanov, *Peterburgskie zimy* [Petersburg Winters], (New York, 1952), pp. 124-128.

the future assassin of the German ambassador, Count Mirbach, was engaged in the macabre task of filling in blank death warrants (already signed by Feliks Dzerzhinskij, the head of the Cheka) with the names of "counter-revolutionaries," which he was drunkenly and haphazardly transferring from other lists. Mandelstam was naturally terrified of the leather-jacketed Bljumkin and his grim task, but, after what one may suppose to have been agonies of resolution, he leaped from his seat, snatched the warrants from Bljumkin's hands, tore them to bits before the astounded gaze of everyone, and raced headlong from the room. Ivanov alleges that Mandelstam told him later that he had wandered about in the snow of that Moscow night, recited poetry, his own and others', smoked, and finally, at dawn, sat on a bench beside the river and wept.

When it finally became light he got up—here the story, already fantastic enough, takes a turn that puts one's powers of belief to the severest test—and went into the Kremlin to the apartment of Kameneva, the sister of Trotsky and the wife of Lev Borisovich Kamenev, one of the most powerful Bolsheviks of the Revolution, where he waited for that lady to wake up. When she did, he was admitted, warmly received, told to wash up, given tea, bundled into the overcoat of Lev Borisovich himself, and taken off by Kameneva for an interview with the signer of the ill-fated death warrants, Feliks Dzerzhinskij. Dzerzhinskij received them at once and, on hearing Kameneva's account of what had happened, thanked the speechless poet who stood before him and ordered into the telephone that Bljumkin be arrested immediately in order to be tried before a summary court within the hour. He then told his visitors that Bljumkin would be shot that same day. Mandelstam, according to Ivanov, attempted to stutter out a plea that Bljumkin be merely exiled and not executed, but Kameneva led him away before he could get it out. She took him to his

apartment, gave him some money, and advised him to remain concealed for at least two days.

Bljumkin was arrested at noon. At two o'clock some
well-wisher telephoned Mandelstam the information that
Bljumkin was free and searching the entire city for him.
At this juncture Mandelstam disappears from our view
as he did, mercifully, from that of Bljumkin.

Once more, whether or not the dramatic *details* of the
foregoing were fabricated by Ivanov, the fact remains that
the essential outline of this story has the independent cor-
roboration of others whose testimony is more reliable. In
addition to the anonymous support which I have already
mentioned, I am told by my colleague Nina Berberova
that Mandelstam's amazing heroism was discussed in Berlin
in 1922 by Il'ja Ehrenburg and Vladislav Khodasevich.

It seems to me that in this curious blend of literature and
reality, the episode of Parnok's attempt to forestall an
unjust execution comes from reality: it is a lightly concealed recapitulation of Mandelstam's moment of reckless
heroism, an event which must have impressed itself deeply
within his consciousness. It has no precedent in the literary
sources, and while not everything in the story must be
assumed to mirror something in art or life, it is true that
we have found the source of most of the important elements,
which must strengthen our confidence that we have found
it in this case, too.

It will be further strengthened by continuing the evidence of the autobiographical nature of *The Egyptian
Stamp*. The entire tone of the story is thoroughly Semitic.
Parnok is a Jew. The "melancholy, bewhiskered silence" in
Jewish apartments is precisely the atmosphere described
in Ivanov's picture of the gloomy meals in the apartment
of Mandelstam's parents.[34] Practically every proper name
encountered is Jewish: Shapiro, Kaplan, Grusenberg, Babel,

[34] *Ibid.*, p. 114.

and so on. Unnamed characters are specified as Jewish; the watchmaker, for instance, is Jewish and resembles Spinoza. Memory is personified as a sick Jewish girl. The contralto of Mme. Mervis flows like Jewish honey. The swarming, shifting, baffling scenes of *The Egyptian Stamp* are, indeed, nothing less than that "Judaic chaos" which Mandelstam portrays in *The Noise of Time*.

But I have called such references to his life "private," for they are revealed only by a special knowledge of Mandelstam's personal life and by the most sedulous collation of his published works. He could hardly have expected his audience to remark the significance of such things as the mention of Ejlers' flower shop on Ofitserskaja. But that he did intend his readers to be aware of the autobiographical elements in *The Egyptian Stamp* is evidenced by a second, more explicit type of reference to himself. The narrator of the story is ubiquitously present, like the ironic and whimsical narrator of Gogol's tales. He refers to his pen (the symbol of the very process that is creating the story before our eyes), which he has some trouble in subordinating to his will, and to the manuscript itself: "Destroy your manuscript, but save whatever you have inscribed in the margin out of boredom, out of helplessness and, as it were, in a dream."[35] The most explicit implication of himself in the whole story is the already noted *cri de coeur*: "Lord! Do not make me like Parnok! Give me the strength to distinguish myself from him." This altogether ironic entreaty is echoed in the still more ironic exclamation: "What a pleasure for a narrator to switch from the third person to the first!" The irony is that he has inserted first-person narration throughout. Such inserted anecdotal reminiscences as those about Shapiro, the sooty lamp, Geshka Rabinovich, Aunt Vera, the little domestic dictionary are all, in the

[35] Berkovskij, p. 176, notes that *The Egyptian Stamp* is stylized

strictest sense, continuations of the autobiography in *The Noise of Time.*

The Egyptian Stamp would thus appear to be, to adopt one of E. M. Forster's phrases for the novel as a genre, "a queer blend of Poetry and History"—not, though, just any poetry and history. Let us ask why this particular poetry—the narrow, though dual, theme from Russian literature to which Mandelstam added his surrealistic extension—and why this particular history, his own and that of his times. Surely the significance of the novella is heightened by the date of its appearance, 1928, and by the time in which it is set, the "Kerenskij summer" of 1917. Like many other men of good will, Mandelstam believed at first in the inevitability of the political upheaval of the Revolution and welcomed it. With negligible exceptions, however, the Revolution left virtually no overt trace on his creative work, a fact which hostile critics never omitted from their charges against him. But one cannot read Mandelstam's poetry—even that written as early as 1918 (e.g., "Sumerki svobody" [The Twilight of Freedom])—without receiving an immediate and clear sense of his overwhelming sadness. I think one may interpret part of the meaning of *The Egyptian Stamp* as Mandelstam's intensely personal protest against what had become of the promise of the Revolution. The pathetic hero, Parnok-Mandelstam, heavy with the literary tradition of which he is emblematic, scurries over the face of his beloved Petersburg in search of more than his clothes: he seeks his very identity and the redemption of a promise that has failed. But this "concert-going" intellectual is at the mercy of a part of himself that has gained power over him, the strutting military officer, Captain Krzyżanowski. In an agony of terror before the frenzied mob and the "maniacal automobiles," he vainly

---

in the manner of a manuscript containing two texts, the second consisting of "marginal notes," the autobiographical asides.

seeks to get in touch with forces that might restore the legitimacy of the past, but he foresees, in a moving and prophetic passage, the very "desolation and abyss" which awaited him.

One senses in the story a rhythmic alternation between the present and the past. The foreground of present time is ringed about with images of horror, while the past is always recalled with affection and longing. The little inserted episode about the death of Angiolina Bosio (p. 182) can serve as a model of this. As the singer is dying, a fire brigade rushes past on the Nevskij with a terrible clangor and din; her guttering consciousness transforms this into the overture of *I due Foscari*, the opera of her London debut, and she lifts herself from her bed in an attempt to respond one last time to her cue. Parnok's inner musing in most cases amounts to just this: a mastery of the unthinkable present by wrapping it round with warm little visions and cultured musings on the past.

An analysis of the remarkable style of *The Egyptian Stamp* falls outside the scope of this brief study, in which my aim has been to deal with the sources of the tale, but at least one of the aspects of that style must claim our attention because of its immediate relevancy to what has just been said.

Mandelstam's novella might serve as a veritable textbook of one of the "devices" of literary art which received its name and formulation in the writings of the Russian Formalist school of criticism: *ostranenie* (making strange). First labeled and analyzed by Viktor Shklovskij, this is a poetic technique for compelling the reader to perceive the familiar external world in a new way. Thus, as Shklovskij pointed out, when Tolstoy in *War and Peace* describes an evening at the opera in the naïve terms of a young girl's vision, without any of the aesthetic sophistication or technical terminology usually associated with such a scene, he renovates our very perception, fatigued by long familiarity, of what we thought we knew.[36]

But Mandelstam's use of *ostranenie* is not that of Tolstoy. Far from presenting the visual world in its primeval state, stripped bare of the accretions of sophisticated terminology, Mandelstam rather increases the complexity and enriches the image of whatever he portrays, "making it strange" by the startling juxtaposition of images from widely different, and usually opposed, areas of life. Thus bast mats are likened to the chasubles of priests; a drawbridge is perceived as a wooden, stone-bound book; the flames of blowtorches are white, shaggy roses; a personified Dawn breaks her colored pencils, which gape like the beaks of nestlings; a page of music is a revolution in an ancient German city. The incongruity of such metaphors, as Berkovskij noted, represents the very essence of Mandelstamian prose style. What Berkovskij did not point out, however, and what it is essential to realize in order to understand the significance of this device for the total meaning of *The Egyptian Stamp*, is that there is a *patterned* selection of the incongruous images that are juxtaposed. Incongruity can be achieved in any number of ways, but Mandelstam achieved it over and over again in only one way, the significance of which must therefore be marked.

To be more specific, in an overwhelming number of instances one component of the incongruity is drawn from a semantic area that can be characterized by the adjectives "massive," "lethal," "threatening," "hot," "revolting," while the other comes from the area of the "frail," "delicate," "cold," "defenseless," "beautiful." Here is a selection of certain contrasts to exemplify what is meant:

pistols fire into chinaware / cold, white flame / white blood / airy outline of Europe: blunt boot of Africa /

[36] See Victor Erlich, *Russian Formalism: History—Doctrine* (The Hague, 1955), p. 150f.

steamship engines checked by roulades and tremolos /
golden vultures rending a singer / tornado sweeping away
a family like a little feather / the lemonade government /
airplane drilling a hole in the azure / irons like battleships
travel over the whipped cream of frilly clothes / mother-of-
pearl filth / scarlatina tree in enema groves / chicken pistons of a locomotive / a railroad station for fat roses /
Parnok is a lemon seed in a crevice of granite / starling
houses in boiling pitch / palaces like silken cowls / the
mummy of a flower / flame of torches lick the mirror /
white bark, tender as a bridal veil / terror in a white
cotton glove.

The omnipresence of this pattern of imagery in the
story is clearly to be identified with the basic dichotomy
which informs *The Egyptian Stamp*. Parnok—the frail,
delicate, utterly defenseless hero—belongs to the same world
of imagery as the bridal veil, silken cowl, flowers, mirrors,
and green branch; while to the other world, the world of
threat and danger, belong Captain Krzyżanowski, the
locomotives, the flames, the tornado, the vultures, battleships, and filth.

If art lives, as the Formalist critic Boris Eichenbaum
wrote, "by interweaving and contrasting its own traditions,
by developing and refashioning them on the principles of
contrast, parody, shifting and sliding,"[37] it is clear that
the meaning of *The Egyptian Stamp* will be in the final
analysis artistic.

Mandelstam was attempting to do what is done success-
fully only in the greatest art: to advance the frontier of
vision by creating something new out of the resources of
a strong tradition. It is our recognition not only of the
familiar tradition in the helpless little figure of Parnok
driven to the edge of madness in his search for identity and

[37] *Skvoz' literaturu* [Through Literature], (Leningrad, 1924),
p. 256.

compassion, but also of what that tradition becomes, how it is transformed in its radically new statement, that lends profound significance to *The Egyptian Stamp.*

· VII ·

As I have indicated, Mandelstam is a unique prose stylist. But since to present any writer in translation is to present him bereft of his style, perhaps some atonement can be made by a few comments on what impression this style makes in the original Russian.

He composed word by word, sentence by sentence, paragraph by paragraph. "Lapidary" as a qualifier of style has lately fallen into disrepute, but it is not one which the author of *Stone* could have rejected. Each of the elements of his prose was carefully polished, hefted for balance, weighed and tested before the next was undertaken. Most paragraphs give the distinct impression of a new start, a fresh adventure, something written in another key. Individual sentences have a grace, rhythm, and wit that render them unforgettable.

For example, the two sentences beginning at the words "Wandering musicians . . ." on page 93 are one in Mandelstam's Russian, and whatever the translation may convey, I ask the reader to believe that the original must have cost its author considerable pain. Nothing comes out this right by accident. The wretched little brass bands wander through Mandelstam's syntax as they did in life, now faster, now slower, now miraculously in time for a few measures, and ending with a fine, brave flourish: ". . . of the splendid Karolina." About his prose as about his poetry there is a peculiar material quality, an almost palpable substance and texture, and this plasticity of his language can often be observed when he renders, as in this sentence, physical movement. In the first paragraph of "The Harbor Master" one reads:

"There beyond the salt marshes there was no longer any starch, there were no washerwomen, no glad subordination, and it would be impossible there to have that springy step, as after a swim, that permanent excitement: the blended sense of well-bought currency, of clear government service and, at the age of forty, the feeling of having passed one's exams." It is a typically Mandelstamian sentence in a number of ways, but it is especially so when the gait of the harbor master is described. In Russian, Mandelstam alliterates on *p*, spaces the ictus with an almost verse-like regularity, and the result is not so much talk about the bouncy step of Sarandinaki as it is a rhythmical imitation of it: "éta poxódka, uprúgaja, kak pósle kupán'ja. . . ." The first sentence of "Mazesa da Vinci" deals with horse-drawn vehicles clattering up the cobblestoned streets of Theodosia and ends with a curious statement which can be translated literally "there were enough hooves for four blocks." But the actual sense of the statement is probably the secondary and not very important result of a little rhyming tune, which caught Mandelstam's fancy to the exclusion of everything else: ". . . kopýt xvatálo na četýre kvartála." It is no accident that, in his essay on Dante, Mandelstam apprehends the rhythmic cadences of the *Divine Comedy* first of all as a literary sublimate of the physical motion of walking:

"The question occurs to me—and quite seriously—how many shoe soles, how many ox-hide soles, how many sandals Alighieri wore out in the course of his poetic work, wandering about on the goat paths of Italy. The *Inferno* and especially the *Purgatorio* glorify the human gait, the measure and rhythm of walking, the foot and its shape. The step, linked to the breathing and saturated with thought: this Dante understands as the beginning of prosody. In order to indicate walking he uses a multitude of varied and charming turns of phrase."[38]

[38] From a copy of the unpublished essay "Razgovor o Dante"

I think that it is in the light of the foregoing that one has to read one of the many asides on literature in *The Egyptian Stamp*:

"The railroad has changed the whole course, the whole structure, the whole rhythm of our prose. It has delivered it over to the senseless muttering of the French moujik out of *Anna Karenina*. Railroad prose, like the woman's purse of that ominous moujik, is full of the coupler's tools, delirious particles, grappling-iron prepositions, and belongs rather among things submitted in legal evidence: it is divorced from any concern with beauty and that which is beautifully rounded."

Does this not reveal one of the principal concerns of Mandelstam as a prosaist? We are to understand the pernicious effect of the railroad, I think, as referring not only to the mechanization of modern life, the distance we have come from simple walking, but to all that beefy, oily, hot massiveness that forever threatened Mandelstam's fragile equilibrium. His prose could never be submitted as legal evidence in any imaginable court, for its aim is beauty and to be beautifully rounded. Its only testimony is to that ineffable satisfaction that comes when sentences wave like flags and strut like peacocks and roll trippingly off the tongue.

A part of the impression of density and close-knittedness, of that plasticity which I am seeking to describe, must certainly come from the associative habits by which Mandelstam proceeded. Words beget words, images beget images. One constantly hears in the mind's ear verbal echoes of what has just preceded. Or, to change the figure, certain images and sounds seem to plop into his prose and propagate ever widening circles.

The second paragraph of "Sergej Ivanych" is dominated

[Conversation about Dante], kindly made available to me by Professor Gleb Struve.

by the image of paper. First men are said to fall into categories of bound paper: books, newspapers, and interlinear translations. Then Sergej Ivanych's cold-stuffed head is said to rustle with pages of flimsy. In Russian, flimsy is called "cigarette paper," and this mention of cigarette leads to a remark about Sergej Ivanych's cigarette, rolled out of illegal paper, and so on.

The fifth chapter of *The Egyptian Stamp* concludes with a rather hallucinatory cacophony of bits of conversation, the author's voice, and disembodied snatches of doggerel. In the midst of it occurs this paragraph: "The January calendar with its ballet goats, its model dairy of myriad worlds, its crackle of a deck of cards being unwrapped. . . ." The word "ballet" appears because this is in the context of talk about *Giselle*, but it is applied to goats because it refers to the saltant image of a goat which is the tenth (or strictly speaking the eleventh) sign of the zodiac, Capricorn, covering the period from December 21 to January 20, and represented on the calendar. A few lines later these associations lead us to the final paragraph, opening with the words "The Petersburg cabby is a myth, a Capricorn. He should be put in the zodiac." In analyzing the means by which the cabby is somehow woven into the web of associations started at the January calendar, we have passed other complex and interlocking elements, such as the dairy summoned up by the goats, and, most remarkable of all, the crackle of the new deck of cards, an image produced not only by its obvious association with the first sheet of a new calendar, but also by the rich mythological links with card playing and even by the sharp wintry sound, as of the snow crust being broken, frequently referred to by Mandelstam.

To be convinced of how thoroughly conscious a device this is, one has only to turn once again to the essay on Dante. It is a characteristic of Mandelstam's criticism and another indication of its wholly personal nature that it often throws at least as much light on his own poetic practice as it does on the subject at hand. In discussing the flight made by Dante and Virgil on the back of the winged monster Geryon in Canto XVII of the *Inferno*, Mandelstam declares it to be a prime example of what he calls the "transformability of poetic material." By this phrase he means the process which we have just been examining: the subtle chain of association and implication which causes one image to give birth to another and that to a third, imparting to the whole a sense, however unconscious, of inevitable rightness and logic.

The impetus of association in Mandelstam's prose springs not only from the sense but also from the sound of the words. Rhyme is heuristic, as the great American linguist Edward Sapir once pointed out,[39] and it can hardly be doubted that Mandelstam was often led to new discoveries of theme and manner by nothing more than the reverberations which particular words set going in his inner ear. The following strange little passage may serve as an intensely concentrated instance of this: "Garbage in the squares . . . Simoom . . . Arabs . . . 'Semën simpered to the proseminar.' " The word for garbage is *músor*. This has a near phonetic identity with *mussón*, which means "monsoon," the seasonal wind of the Indian Ocean and southern Asia which alters its direction according to the time of year. *Mussón* itself, however, is one of those temporary bridges of thought which Mandelstam was forever burning behind him. It does not appear in the text. What does appear is its influence in prompting the association with another wind, the *samúm* (simoom), the pestilential, sand-laden wind of the Arabian desert. Hence—*araby* (Arabs). The consonantal structure of *samúm* is such that it produces in turn its near phonic relative, the proper name *Semën*, and this cues the pyrotechnic

---

[39] "The Heuristic Value of Rhyme," *Selected Writings of Edward Sapir in Language, Culture and Personality* (Berkeley and Los Angeles, 1951), pp. 496-499.

punning of the final sentence: *Prosemenil Semën v prose-minarij.* (See n. 66, p. 200.)

In the following passage, a resemblance in sound has again pointed the way for the sense to follow: "Pust' trudnejšie passaži Lista, razmaxivaja kostyljami, *volok*ut tuda i obratno požarnuju lestnicu. Rojal'—éto umnyj i dobryj komnatnyj zver' s *volok*nistym derevjannym mjas-om. . . ." (Let the most difficult passages of Liszt, waving their crutches about, *drag* the fire ladder there and back. The grand piano is an intelligent and good-natured house animal with *fibrous*, wooden flesh. . . .) Between these two words there does exist a distant etymological relationship, but one can be confident that it was the sound alone which prompted this connection.

There are many examples of such association in the pages of Mandelstam. I will mention one more. In the first paragraph of "The Concerts of Hofmann and Kubelik" there is a sentence that goes "I can recall no other musical experiences . . . that might be compared with these *Lenten* orgies in the *white-columned* hall." In Russian, the italicized words read: "s étimi *velikopóstnymi* órgijami v *belokolón-nom* zále." The words *velikopóstnyj* and *belokolónnyj* are, in the first place, of similar morphological construction, being compounds of modifier plus substantive plus adjectival suffix, and they are also in similar syntactic position. They are identical in stress pattern: - - - ′ -. Finally, and most importantly, these identities are supported by an alternation of vowel and consonant which causes the second word to be perceived by the reader as a kind of phonic shadow of the first. I am speaking, of course, of the pronunciation. In ordinary prose, such repetitions would be avoided, but Mandelstam's prose subsists on the flourish, the almost physical gesture of this and similar passages.

As a miniaturist and digressionary, Mandelstam stands in the tradition of Gogol. His poetic gift for condensation and precise observation can be seen in his skill at making a few lightning strokes of narrative shorthand render up a complete little story:

"Somewhere in the Ile de France: grape barrels, white roads, poplars—and a winegrower has set out with his daughters to go to their grandmother in Rouen. On his return he is to find everything 'scellé,' the presses and vats under an official seal, the doors and cellars closed with sealing wax. The manager had tried to conceal from the excise tax collectors a few pails of new wine. They had caught him in the act. The family is ruined. Enormous fine. And, as a result, the stern laws of France make me the present of a governess."

This surefooted little paragraph moves without a single false step through a tangled growth of incident and scene and comes out—to our surprise—at the place where it had started: an account of the French governesses and maids whom he knew as a child.

Such narrative asides are frequent, and give to the pattern of Mandelstam's prose an effect of mosaic and montage. Mandelstam uses this technique not only in his larger composition but also in individual sentences. Thus the "chaos of Judaism" is pieced together for us in a mosaic sentence: "The chaos of Judaism showed through all the chinks of the stone-clad Petersburg apartment: in the threat of ruin, in the cap hanging in the room of the guest from the provinces, in the spiky script of the unread books of Genesis, thrown into the dust one shelf lower than Goethe and Schiller, in the shreds of the black-and-yellow ritual." And it is sharply contrasted with the Russian reality surrounding it in the next sentence, which turns out to be another mosaic: "The strong, ruddy, Russian year rolled through the calendar with decorated eggs, Christmas trees, steel skates from Finland, December, gaily bedecked Finnish cabdrivers, and the villa."

In the different employment of this technique we can see one of the principal differences between *The Noise of*

Time and *The Egyptian Stamp*, for in the latter the process of disintegration has greatly advanced, the individual pieces of the mosaic tend to be smaller, less uniform, and more widely spaced. In fact, were it not for the hopelessly pejorative sense attaching to the word, the most appropriate term for this aspect of Mandelstam's style would be "decadence," for it is precisely the tendency toward decomposition that Paul Bourget saw as the fundamental element in the decadent style: "Un style de décadence est celui où l'unité du livre se décompose pour laisser la place à l'indépendance de la page, où la page se décompose pour laisser la place à l'indépendance de la phrase, et la phrase pour laisser la place à l'indépendance du mot."[40]

This is not at all to say that the totality of the impression is diffuse. However lavish the attention which Mandelstam devoted to individual words, phrases, and pages, these elements unite at last to leave the reader with a vision of reality that is single and whole. The experience transfigured in these chapters of lightly fictionalized memoirs and documentary fiction is of course not external, but how vividly is the inner life of an epoch, the *noise* heard in the mind, made to live in our own imaginations! There are many accounts of what took place in the external Petrograd of the Kerenskij summer; Mandelstam's novella transmits the inner experience of the death of Russian culture. Relatives and bystanders may have that circumstantial and detailed knowledge of a man's death which is commonly accredited as real, but the dying man himself, as Emily Dickinson knew, is bemused by the buzz of a fly.

In Soviet parlance, of course, decadence is a standard term of abuse, and though the critic M. Vitenson did not use it, he had in mind something like Bourget's definition when he wrote the following sinister paragraph in 1934: "Criticism must realize that the artistic method of isolating

[40] *Oeuvres complètes* (Paris, 1899), I, 15f.

the events represented, an isolation that consists of separating the part from the whole, such as is now practiced by certain writers (K. Vaginov, V. Shklovskij, O. Mandelstam), leads to a distortion of reality. This method . . . is a new tactic of the class enemy in literature."[41]

One of Mandelstam's essays has acquired, in consequence of his hard fate, a peculiar poignancy. This is the one entitled "O sobesednike" (On the Interlocutor), where he confronts a problem that is central to every writer: that of the audience. His conclusion is that a poet must out of necessity address himself to some future reader. It is impossible to be truly free if one is fettered by the knowledge that some particular, familiar, contemporary audience is listening. Only by addressing his unknown, merely presumptive reader in posterity is the poet able to achieve that continuous sense of surprise which Mandelstam saw as the essential ingredient of all true art. Though Mandelstam also wrote, in one of his later poems, "I will be inclosed in some alien speech," it is hardly likely that he could have expected to be speaking, after a lapse of some forty years, to the readers of this book and in their own language. But it was in the same essay that he himself observed how providential is the force that drives the mariner's message in its glass bottle across no matter how wide a sea into the hands of the one who is destined to find it.

[41] M. Vitenson, "O 'pravde žizni,' o klassovoj bor'be v literature i o zadačax kritiki" [On "The Truth of Life," the Class Struggle in Literature, and the Tasks of Criticism], *Zvezda* [Star], 2 (1934), 171.

The Noise of Time

1925

A.B. 1912.

Music in Pavlovsk

I REMEMBER well the remote and desolate years[1] of Russia, the decade of the nineties, slowly slipping past in their unhealthy tranquillity and deep provincialism—a quiet backwater: the last refuge of a dying age. At morning tea there would be talk about Dreyfus, there were the names of Colonels Esterhazy and Picquart, vague disputes about some "Kreutzer Sonata" and, behind the high podium of the glass railroad station in Pavlovsk,[2] the change of conductors, which seemed to me a change of dynasties. Immobile newsboys on the corners, without cries, without movements, awkwardly rooted to the sidewalk—narrow droshkies with a little collapsible seat for a third passenger —and, all in all, I picture the nineties in my mind in scenes scattered apart but inwardly bound together by the quiet misery and the painful, doomed provincialism of the life that was dying.

The ladies' wide bouffant sleeves, luxuriously puffed-up at the shoulders and pulled tight at the elbows, and their wasp waists; the moustaches, imperials, carefully trimmed beards; men's faces and haircuts such as one could find now only in the portrait gallery of some run-down barbershop where there are pictures of the "Capoul cut" and the "coq."

What, in a word, were the nineties? Ladies' bouffant sleeves and music in Pavlovsk: the balloons of the ladies' sleeves and all the rest revolve around the glass railroad station in Pavlovsk, and Galkin,[3] the conductor, stands at the center of the world.

In the middle of the nineties all Petersburg streamed into Pavlovsk as into some Elysium. Locomotive whistles and railroad bells mingled with the patriotic cacophony of the *1812 Overture*, and a peculiar smell filled the huge station where Tchaikovsky and Rubinstein reigned. The humid air from the mouldy parks, the odor of the decaying hotbeds and hothouse roses—this was blended with the heavy exhalations from the buffet, the acrid smoke of cigars, a burning smell from somewhere in the station, and the cosmetics of the crowd of many thousands.

As it turned out, we became "winter people" in Pavlovsk, that is, we lived the year round in our *dacha* in that old ladies' town, that Russian demi-Versailles, the city of court lackeys, widows of high officials, redheaded policemen, consumptive pedagogues (it was thought more salubrious to live in Pavlovsk) and grafters who had raked together enough money for a detached villa. O, those years—when Figner[4] was losing his voice and the double caricature of him passed around from hand to hand: on one side he was singing and on the other stopping up his ears. When carefully bound volumes of *The Field, Universal Virgin Soil*, and the *Foreign Literature Herald*, crushing book stands and card tables beneath their weight, were to constitute for a long time to come the basis of the libraries of the petty bourgeoisie.

There are nowadays no encyclopedias of science and technology like those bound monsters. But the *Universal Panoramas* and *Virgin Soils* were true fonts of knowledge of the world. I loved the "miscellany" about ostrich eggs, two-headed calves, and festivals in Bombay and Calcutta, and especially the pictures, the huge, full-page pictures: Malayan swimmers bound to boards and skimming through waves the size of a three-storied house; the mysterious experiment of a M. Fouqué: a metal sphere with an enormous pendulum skimming around it in the midst of a throng of serious gentlemen wearing neckties and pointed beards. I have a feeling that the grownups read the same thing as I, that is, mainly the supplements, the immense, burgeoning literature of the supplements to *The Field* and the rest. Our interests were, in general, identical, and at the age of seven or eight I was fully abreast of the century. More and more often I heard the expression *fin de siècle*, the end of the century, repeated with frivolous hauteur and with a sort of coquettish melancholy. It was as if, having acquitted Dreyfus and settled accounts with Devil's Island, that strange century had lost all meaning.

It is my impression that the men were exclusively absorbed day and night by the Dreyfus affair, while the women—that is, the ladies with the bouffant sleeves—hired and fired the servants, an activity that provided inexhaustible food for lively and delightful conversations.

On Nevskij Prospekt in the building of the Roman Catholic Church of St. Catherine there lived a respectable little old man named père Lagrange. One of the functions of His Reverence was to recommend poor young French girls who were seeking positions as governesses in respectable houses. Ladies came to consult père Lagrange straight from the Gostinyj Dvor[5] with their parcels in their hands. He would come out in his decrepit way, wearing his shabby cassock, and affectionately banter the children with unctuous Catholic jokes, spiced with French wit. The recommendations of père Lagrange were taken very seriously.

The famous employment office for cooks, nursemaids, and governesses on Vladimir Street, to which I was rather often taken along, resembled a genuine slave market. Those who were looking for a place were led out in turn. The ladies sniffed them over and asked to see their references. The recommendation of some totally unknown lady, especially if it were the wife of a general, was regarded as sufficiently weighty; but it sometimes happened that the creature who had been led out for sale, having carefully examined the buyer, would make a rude noise right in her face and walk away. Then the intermediary in this slave traffic would come running up with apologies and talk about the decline of manners.

Once again I glance back at Pavlovsk and take morning strolls through all the walks and parquets of the station, where over a foot of confetti and serpentin has collected overnight—remnants of the storm which used to be called a "benefit performance." Kerosene lamps were being converted to electricity. The horsecars still ran along the streets of Petersburg behind stumbling nags out of *Don Quixote*. Along Goroxovaja as far as the Alexander Garden one could see the *karetka*, the most ancient form of public vehicle in Petersburg. Only on the Nevskij could one hear the clanging bells of the new express trams, painted yellow rather than the usual dirty wine color, and drawn by enormous, sleek horses.

· II ·

Childish Imperialism

The equestrian statue of Nicholas I across from the State Council Building was guarded by a grenadier, mossy with age, who would march in a ceaseless circle around it, winter and summer, with a shaggy sheepskin cap pulled down over one eye. His headdress resembled a mitre and was practically as large as a whole sheep.

We children would strike up conversations with this decrepit sentry. It was a disappointment to learn that he was not, as we had thought, a veteran of 1812. But he informed us that the other old codgers like himself were sentries, the last to have served under Nicholas, and that in the entire company there remained only about five or six of them.

The entrances to the Summer Garden—both the one near the river, where the railing and the chapel are located, and the one across from the Engineers' Palace[6]—were guarded by cavalry sergeant majors bedecked with medals. They determined whether a person was suitably dressed. Men in Russian boots they drove away, nor would they admit persons in caps or in the attire of the lower middle class. The manners of the children in the Summer Garden were extremely ceremonious. After a whispered consultation with a governess or nurse, some bare-legged child would approach the park bench and, after a bow or a curtsey, would pipe, "Little girl (or little boy—such was the official form of address), would you not like to play 'London Bridge' or 'Hide and Seek'?"

After such a beginning, you can imagine how merry the game was. I never played, and the very etiquette of introductions struck me as forced.

As it turned out, I spent my early childhood in Petersburg under the sign of the most authentic militarism, but it was really not my fault: it was the fault of my nurse and of the Petersburg street of that period.

We would take our walks along the deserted stretch of Bol'shaja Morskaja Street, where one finds the red Lutheran church and the wood-paved embankment of the Mojka.

Thus we imperceptibly approached the Krjukov Canal, the Dutch Petersburg of ships' berths and Neptune arches with marine emblems, and the barracks of the crew of marine guardsmen.

Here on the green roadway over which no vehicles ever passed, the marine guards held their drills, and the brass kettledrums and the drums shook the waters of the quiet canal. I liked the physical selection of the men—they were all taller than the normal height—and my nurse completely shared my tastes. Thus we selected one sailor, the "black moustache," as we called him, came regularly to

look at him personally, and, when we had picked him out
of the formation, would not take our eyes off him till the
end of the exercises. And I say now, without a moment's
hesitation, that at the age of seven or eight all this—the
whole massif of Petersburg, the granite and wood-paved
quarters, all the gentle heart of the city with its overflow
of squares, its shaggy parks, its islands of monuments, the
caryatids of the Hermitage, the mysterious Millionnaja
Street, where there were no passers-by and where only one
small grocery store had wormed itself in among the marble,
but especially the General Staff Arch, the Senate Square,
and all Dutch Petersburg I regarded as something sacred
and festive.

I do not know with what imaginary inhabitants the
fancy of young Romans used to people their capital, but
as for me, I filled these fortresses and squares with a sort
of unthinkably ideal, universal, military parade.

It is characteristic that I did not for a moment believe
in the Kazan Cathedral, for all the tobacco twilight of its
vaults or its forest of bullet-riddled banners.[7]

That place was also unusual, but of it more later. The
stone horseshoe of the colonnade and the wide paved court
with its guard chains were meant for riots, and for my
imagination this place had no less interest and significance
than the May Parade on the Field of Mars. What will the
weather be like? Won't they put it off? Will it even take
place this year? But they have already laid out boards and
planks along the Summer Canal, the carpenters are already hammering on the Field of Mars, and the grand-
stands are already swelling up like mountains, dust is
roiling over the mock attacks, and the infantrymen, spaced
apart like stakes in the ground, wave their banners. The
platform was erected in about three days. Such rapid construction seemed to me miraculous, and the dimensions
of it overwhelmed me like the Coliseum. I visited the site
daily, marveled at the graceful ease of the work, ran up

and down the stairs feeling as if I were on the stage, a participant in the next day's splendid spectacle, and envied the very boards themselves, which would probably see the attack.

If one could only hide in the Summer Garden unnoticed! There would be the Babylonian uproar of hundreds of orchestras, the field, sprouting bayonets like ears of corn, the acreage patterns of the formations of foot and horse, as if they were not regiments but standing fields of buckwheat, rye, oats, and barley. The covert movement between the regiments along the interior clearings in the ranks. And more—the silver trumpets, the bugles, the bedlam of shouts, drums, and kettledrums. To see the attack of the cavalry!

It always seemed to me that in Petersburg something very splendid and solemn was absolutely bound to happen.

I was in ecstasy when the lanterns were draped in black crepe and black ribbons were strung up on the occasion of the death of the heir to the throne. The mounting of the guard at the Alexander Column, the funeral pomps of some general, the "progress"—such were my daily diversions.

"Progress" was the name then used for the trips of the Czar and his family through the streets. I acquired great proficiency in learning of these events beforehand. At the Anichkov Palace at a certain time members of the palace constabulary would come crawling out like red mustachioed cockroaches: "Nothing special, ladies and gentlemen. Move along, please. . . ." But the house porters were already scattering yellow sand with their wooden scoops, the constables' moustaches had been dyed, and along Karavannaja and Konjushennaja policemen had been spilled like peas.

It amused me to overwhelm the guards with questions about who was going to come out, and when, but they never dared to tell. I must say that the fleeting glimpse of the emblazoned carriage with the little golden birds on the lanterns or of the English sleigh drawn by trotters covered with nets always left me disappointed. The game of the "progress" seemed to me, nevertheless, rather fun.

The Petersburg street awakened in me a craving for spectacle, and the very architecture of the city inspired me with a kind of childish imperialism: I was delirious over the cuirasses of the Royal Horse Guard and the Roman helmets of the Cavalry Guard, the silver trumpets of the Preobrazhenskij band; and after the May Parade, my favorite distraction was the regimental festival of the Royal Horse Guard on Lady Day.

I also remember the launching of the battleship *Osljabja*, its sliding like some monstrous sea caterpillar down into the water, the cranes, and the ribs of the covered slip.

All this mass of militarism and even a kind of police aesthetics may very well have been proper to some son of a corps commander with the appropriate family traditions, but it was completely out of keeping with the kitchen fumes of a middle-class apartment, to father's study, heavy with the odor of leathers, kidskin and calfskin, or to Jewish conversations about business.

....

· III ·

Riots and French Governesses

....

It was always known in advance when the students would riot in front of the Kazan Cathedral. Every family had its student informer. The result was that these riots were attended—at a respectful distance, to be sure—by a great mass of people: children with their nurses, mamas and aunts who had been unable to keep their insurrectionaries at home, old civil servants, and simply people who happened to be walking idly about. On the day appointed for the riot the sidewalks of the Nevskij teemed with a dense throng of spectators all the way from Sadovaja to the Anichkov Bridge. This mob was afraid to approach the Kazan Cathedral. The police were hidden in courtyards— for example, in the courtyard of the Roman Catholic Church of St. Catherine. The Kazan Square was itself relatively empty; across it would pass small knots of students and actual working men, the latter being pointed at with fingers. Suddenly, from the direction of the Kazan Square, there would burst forth a protracted, crescendoing yell, something on the order of a steady "oo" or "ee," which became an ominous howling, growing nearer and nearer. At that moment the spectators scattered and the crowd was crushed back by the horses. "Cossacks! Cossacks!"— the cry spread like lightning, faster than the Cossacks themselves. The "riot" itself, strictly speaking, was cordoned off and led away to the Mikhajlovskij Manège, and the Nevskij emptied as if it had been swept with a broom.

My first conscious, sharp perceptions were of gloomy crowds of people in the streets. I was exactly three years old. It was 1894 and I had been brought from Pavlovsk to Petersburg for the purpose of seeing the funeral of Alexander III. Furnished rooms had been taken on the fourth floor of some house on the Nevskij, opposite Nikolaevskaja Street. On the evening of the day before the ceremonies, having crawled up on the windowsill and seen the crowd-darkened street, I asked "When will they start?" and was told "tomorrow." It profoundly impressed me that all these throngs of people were spending the entire night in the street. Even death first appeared to me in a totally unnatural, elegant, and festive guise. Once I was walking with Mother and my nurse on the street along the Mojka past the chocolate building of the Italian Embassy. Suddenly the doors there were wide open and everyone was freely admitted inside, and there issued forth a smell of resin, incense, and something sweet and pleasant. Black velvet was draped over the entrance and the walls, which glistened with silver and tropical plants. Very high on his bier lay the embalmed Italian ambassador. What had all that to do with me? I do not know, but these impressions were strong and clear and I cherish them to this day.

The ordinary life of the city was poor and monotonous. Every day at about five o'clock there was promenading on the Bol'shaja Morskaja from Gorokhovaja Street to the General Staff Arch. All the foppish and idle elements of the city then proceeded slowly back and forth along the sidewalks bowing and exchanging smiles: the ring of spurs, the languages of England and France—a living exhibit from the English Store and the Jockey Club. Hither also the nursemaids and governesses, young-looking French-women, brought the children, in order to sigh and compare it all to the Champs Élysées.

So many French governesses were hired to look after me that all their features have become blurred and resolved into one general patch of portraiture. It is my opinion that the little songs, models of penmanship, anthologies, and conjugations had ended by driving all these French and Swiss women themselves into an infantile state. At the center of their world view, distorted by anthologies, stood the figure of the great emperor Napoleon and the War of 1812; after that came Joan of Arc (one Swiss girl, however, turned out to be a Calvinist), and no matter how often I tried, curious as I was, to learn something from them about France, I learned nothing at all, save that it was beautiful. The French governesses placed great value upon the art of speaking fast and abundantly and the Swiss upon the learning of little songs, among which the chief favorite was the "Song of Malbrough." These poor girls were completely imbued with the cult of great men—Hugo, Lamartine, Napoleon, and Molière. On Sundays they had permission to go to mass. They were not allowed to have acquaintances.

Somewhere in the Ile de France: grape barrels, white

roads, poplars—and a winegrower has set out with his daughters to go to their grandmother in Rouen. On his return he is to find everything "scellé," the presses and vats under an official seal, the doors and cellars closed with sealing wax. The manager had tried to conceal from the excise tax collectors a few pails of new wine. They had caught him in the act. The family is ruined. Enormous fine. And, as a result, the stern laws of France make me the present of a governess.

But what had I to do with the Guards' festivals, the monotonous prettiness of the host of the infantry and its steeds, the stone-faced battalions flowing with hollow tread down the Millionnaja, gray with marble and granite?

All the elegant mirage of Petersburg was merely a dream, a brilliant covering thrown over the abyss, while round about there sprawled the chaos of Judaism—not a motherland, not a house, not a hearth, but precisely a chaos, the unknown womb world whence I had issued, which I feared, about which I made vague conjectures and fled, always fled.

The chaos of Judaism showed through all the chinks of the stone-clad Petersburg apartment: in the threat of ruin, in the cap hanging in the room of the guest from the provinces, in the spiky script of the unread books of Genesis, thrown into the dust one shelf lower than Goethe and Schiller, in the shreds of the black-and-yellow ritual.

The strong, ruddy, Russian year rolled through the calendar with decorated eggs, Christmas trees, steel skates from Finland, December, gaily bedecked Finnish cabdrivers, and the villa. But mixed up with all this there was a phantom—the new year in September—and the strange, cheerless holidays, grating upon the ear with their harsh names: Rosh Hashana and Yom Kippur.

The Bookcase

As a little bit of musk fills an entire house, so the least influence of Judaism overflows all of one's life. O, what a strong smell that is! Could I possibly not have noticed that in real Jewish houses there was a different smell from that in Aryan houses? And it was not only the kitchen that smelled so, but the people, things, and clothing. To this day I remember how that sweetish Jewish smell swaddled me in the wooden house of my grandfather and grandmother on Kljuchevaja Street in German Riga. My father's study at home was itself unlike the granite paradise of my sedate strolls; it led one away into an alien world, and the mixture of its furnishings, the selection of the objects in it were strongly knitted together in my consciousness. First of all, there was the hand-made oak armchair bearing the image of a balalaika and a gauntlet and, on its arched back, the motto "Slow but Sure"—a tribute to the pseudo-Russian style of Alexander III. Then there was a Turkish divan completely overwhelmed with ledgers, whose pages of flimsy paper were covered over with the minuscule gothic hand of German commercial correspondence. At first I thought my father's occupation consisted of printing his flimsy letters by cranking the handle of the copying machine. To this day I conceive of the smell of the yoke of labor as the penetrating smell of tanned leather; and the webbed kidskins thrown about the floor, and the pudgy chamois skins with excrescences like living fingers—all this, plus the bourgeois writing table with its little marble calendar, swims in a tobacco haze and is seasoned with the smells of leather. And in the drab surroundings of this mercantile room there was a little glass-front bookcase behind a curtain of green taffeta. It is about that bookcase that I should like to speak now. The bookcase of early childhood is a man's companion for life. The arrangement of its shelves, the choice of books, the colors of the spines are for him the color, height, and arrangement of world literature itself. And as for books which were not included in that first bookcase—they were never to force their way into the universe of world literature. Every book in the first bookcase is, willy-nilly, a classic, and not one of them can ever be expelled.

There was nothing haphazard in the way that strange little library had been deposited, like a geological bed, over several decades. The paternal and maternal elements in it were not mixed, but existed separately, and a cross section of the strata showed the history of the spiritual efforts of the entire family, as well as the inoculation of it with alien blood.

I always remember the lower shelf as chaotic: the books were not standing upright side by side but lay like ruins: reddish five-volume works with ragged covers, a Russian history of the Jews written in the clumsy, shy language of a Russian-speaking Talmudist. This was the Judaic chaos thrown into the dust. This was the level to which my Hebrew primer, which I never mastered, quickly fell. In a fit of national contrition they went as far as hiring a real Jewish teacher for me. He came from his Torgovaja Street and taught without taking off his cap, which made me feel awkward. His correct Russian sounded false. The Hebrew primer was illustrated with pictures which showed one and the same little boy, wearing a visored cap and with a melancholy adult face, in all sorts of situations—with a cat, a book, a pail, a watering can. I saw nothing of myself in that boy and with all my being revolted against the book and the subject. There was one striking thing in that teacher, although it sounded unnatural: the feeling of national Jewish pride. He talked about Jews as the French governess talked about Hugo and Napoleon. But I knew that he hid his pride when he went out into the street, and therefore did not believe him.

Above these Jewish ruins there began the orderly arrangement of books; those were the Germans—Schiller, Goethe, Kerner, and Shakespeare in German—in the old Leipzig and Tübingen editions, chubby little butterballs in stamped claret-colored bindings with a fine print calculated for the sharp vision of youth and with soft engravings done in a rather classical style: women with their hair down wring their hands, the lamp is always shown as an oil lamp, the horsemen have high foreheads, and the vignettes are clusters of grapes. All this was my father fighting his way as an autodidact into the German world out of the Talmudic wilds.

Still higher were my mother's Russian books—Pushkin in Isakov's 1876 edition. I still think that was a splendid edition and like it more than the one published by the Academy. It contained nothing superfluous, the type was elegantly arranged, the columns of poetry flowed freely as soldiers in flying battalions, and leading them like generals were the clear reasonable years of composition, right up to 1837. The color of Pushkin? Every color is accidental—what color could one choose for the purl of speech? O, that idiotic alphabet of colors by Rimbaud . . . !

My Isakov Pushkin was in a cassock of no color at all, in a binding of schoolboy calico, in a brownish-black, faded cassock with a tinge of earth and sand; he feared neither spots, nor ink, nor fire, nor kerosene. For a quarter of a century the black .and sand cassock had lovingly absorbed everything into itself—so vividly do I sense the everyday spiritual beauty, the almost physical charm of my mother's Pushkin. It bore an inscription in reddish ink: "For her diligence as a pupil of the Third Form." The Isakov Pushkin is bound up with stories about ideal schoolmasters and schoolmistresses, ruddy with consumption and shod in ragged boots: the 1880's in Vilno. The word "intellectual" was pronounced by my mother, and especially by my grandmother, with pride. Lermontov had a greenish-blue binding with something military about it: not for nothing was he a hussar. He never seemed to me to be the brother or relative of Pushkin. Goethe and Schiller I regarded as twins, but in Pushkin and Lermontov I recognized two men alien to each other and consciously kept them apart. After 1837, blood and poetry both rang differently in the ears.

And how about Turgenev and Dostoevsky? Those were supplements to *The Field*. In external aspect they were identical, like brothers. They were bound in boards covered with a thin leather. Prohibition lay upon Dostoevsky like a gravestone: it was said that he was "heavy." Turgenev was altogether sanctioned and open, with his Baden-Baden, *Spring Torrents*, and languid conversations. But I knew that the tranquil life in Turgenev had already vanished and was nowhere to be found.

Would you like to know the key to the epoch, the book which had positively become white-hot from handling, the book that would not under any circumstances agree to die, that lay like someone alive in the narrow coffin of the 1890's, the book whose leaves, perhaps from reading or from having been left in the sun on a bench at someone's *dacha*, had yellowed prematurely, whose first page bore the features of a youth with an inspired arrangement of the hair, features that became an icon? Gazing into the face of the young Nadson, I am astonished by the genuine fieriness of those features and at the same time by their total inexpressiveness, their almost wooden simplicity. Does this not describe the whole book? Does it not describe the era? Send him off to Nice, show him the Mediterranean: he will go on singing his ideal and his suffering generation—with the possible addition of a seagull and the crest of a wave. Do not laugh at Nadsonism: it is the enigma of Russian culture and the essentially uncomprehended sound of it, for we do not understand and hear as they understood and heard. Who is he, this wooden monk with the inexpressive features of an eternal youth, this inspired idol of students—especially of students, that is to say, the elite of certain decades—this prophet of school recitals? How many times, knowing already that Nadson was bad, have I still reread his book and, putting away the poetic haughtiness of the present and pity for the ignorance of this youth in the past, tried to hear it as it sounded to his generation. How greatly was I aided in this by the diaries and letters of Nadson: the continual literary drudgery, the candles, applause, the burning faces; the tight ring of his generation and, in the center, the altar—the lecturer's table and its glass of water. Like summer insects above the hot globe of a lamp, an entire generation was carbonized and scorched by the flame of literary celebrations with garlands of allegorical roses, enormous assemblies which bore the character of a cult and expiatory offering for the generation. Hither came those who wished to share the fate of their generation right up to the point of ruin—the haughty ones remained to one side with Tjutchev and Fet. Actually, all that was serious in Russian literature turned away from this consumptive generation with its ideal and its Baal. What was left to it? Paper roses, the candles of the school recitals, and the barcarole of Rubinstein. The 1880's in Vilno as mother recalled them. It was everywhere the same: sixteen-year-old girls tried to read John Stuart Mill and at public recitals one could see luminous personalities who—with a certain dense admixture of pedal, a fainting away on the *piano* passage, and blank features—played the latest things of the leonine Anton. But what actually happened was that the intelligentsia with Buckle and Rubinstein and led by the luminous personalities—who in their beatific idiocy had completely lost the way—resolutely turned to the practice of self-burning. Like high tar-coated torches the adherents of the People's

Will Party burned for all the people to see, with Sofija Perovskaja and Zheljabov,[8] and all of them, all of provincial Russia and all of the students, smouldered in sympathy: not one single green leaf was to be left.

What a meager life, what poor letters, what un-funny jokes and parodies! I used to have pointed out to me in the family album a daguerreotype of my uncle Misha, a melancholiac with swollen and unhealthy features, and it was explained that he had not merely gone out of his mind—he had "burnt up," as that generation put it. They said the same of Garshin, and many were the deaths reduced to that single ritual.

Semën Afanas'ich Vengerov, a relative of mine on my mother's side (the family in Vilno and school memories), understood nothing in Russian literature and studied Pushkin as a professional task, but "one thing" he understood. His "one thing" was: the heroic character of Russian literature. He was a fine one with his heroic character when he would drag slowly along Zagorodnyj Prospekt from his apartment to the card catalog, hanging on the elbow of his aging wife and smirking into his dense ant beard.

··

· V ·

Finland

··

The little red bookcase with the green curtain and the armchair with the motto "Slow but Sure" often moved from apartment to apartment. They stood on Maximilian Lane—where, at the end of the arrow-straight Voznesenskij Prospekt, one could see the galloping statue of Nicholas—and above Ejlers' Flower Shop on Ofitserskaja Street not far from *A Life for the Tsar*, and on Zagorodnyj Prospekt. In the winter, at Christmastime, there was Finland, Vyborg, and the *dacha* at Terioki. At Terioki there was sand, juni-per, little plank walkways, kennel-like bathing houses[9] with carved hearts (and notches to show the number of baths), and our own domestic foreigners, so dear to the heart of the Petersburger, the cold Finns, lovers of the tarred barrels lighted on the Eve of St. John and the trained bears on the lawn of the Narodnyj Dom,[10] the "unshaven and green-eyed" Finns, as Blok called them. From Vladimir Solov'ëv to Blok, pre-revolutionary Petersburg was redolent of Fin-land, sifting its sand from one hand to the other, rubbing its granite forehead with the light Finnish snow, and listening in its deep delirium to the sleighbells of the squat Finnish horses. I always had a troubled intimation of the special meaning which, for a Petersburger, resided in Fin-land: people drove there in order to think to the end what could not be thought to the end in Petersburg, pulling the low snowy sky down to their very eyebrows and dozing off in small hotels where the water in the pitcher was icy. And I loved the country where all the women are immaculate laundresses and the drivers of the horsecabs resemble sen-ators.

In the summertime at Terioki there were entertainments for the children. How stupid those were, when one thinks of it! Small boys from the Gymnasium and military school in their tight-fitting jackets, bowing and scraping before full-grown maidens, would dance the *pas de quatre* and the *pas de patineur*, the salon dances of the nineties, with constrained, expressionless movements. Then came games: a sack-race with an egg—that is, with the legs tied up in a sack and with a raw egg balanced on a wooden spoon. In the lottery it was always a cow that was raffled off. What a joy that was for the French governesses! This was the only place where they twittered like heavenly birds and grew young again in spirit, but the children were lost and con-fused in such strange amusements.

We would go to Vyborg to visit the Sharikovs, a family of merchants who had lived there for a long time. They were descended from the Jewish soldiers in the army of Nicholas, a fact which permitted them to reside legally in Finland, otherwise free of Jews. The Sharikovs—Shariks in Finnish—operated a large shop where they sold Finnish wares—*Sekkatawaaran kauppa*—and where there was an odor of resin, leather, and bread—the special smell of a Finnish shop—and many nails and groats. The Sharikovs lived in a massive wooden house with oak furniture. Our host was especially proud of a sideboard with carvings showing the history of Ivan the Terrible. They ate so much that one could hardly rise from the table. Old Sharikov swam in fat, like Buddha, and spoke with a Finnish accent. One of his daughters—a plain, dark girl—sat behind the counter, and the other three, who were beautiful, ran away in turn with officers of the local garrison. The house smelled of cigars and money. Mme. Sharikov was uneducated and kind, and her guests, army officers, were lovers of punch and good sleighs and all of them card players to the marrow of their bones. After the thinnish atmosphere of Petersburg I rejoiced in this stable, oaken family. I landed willy-nilly in the very thick of the frosty winter flirtations of the high-bosomed Vyborg beauties. Somewhere in Fazer's pastry shop with its vanilla wafers and its chocolate, and behind the blue windows the crunch of sleigh runners and the mad jingle of the bells: having been shaken right out of a fast, narrow sleigh and into the warm steam of a rich Finnish coffeehouse, I witnessed the immodest argument of a desperate young lady with an army lieutenant over whether or not he was wearing a corset, and I remember how he swore by God and proposed that she feel his ribs through his tunic. Swift sleighs, punch, cards, a Swedish toy fortress of cardboard, the Swedish language, military music —the Vyborg intoxication was dispersed by the little blue flame on the punch. The Hotel Belvedere, where the First

Duma later held its meetings, was famed for its cleanliness and for its snow-cold, blindingly white bed linen. Everything was here—a foreign air and Swedish coziness. The stubborn and crafty little town with its coffee mills, rocking chairs, worsted wool carpets, and Bible verses carved in the headboard of every bed bore the yoke of Russian militarism like the scourge of God. But in every house there hung, in a frame of mourning black, a picture of a bareheaded girl named Suomi, above whose head there bristled the angry two-headed eagle while she fiercely clasped to her breast a book with the label—*Law*.

· VI ·

The Judaic Chaos

There once arrived at our house a person completely unknown to us, an unmarried lady of about forty, in a little red hat and with a sharp chin and angry dark eyes. On the strength of her having come from the small town of Shavli, she demanded that we find her a husband in Petersburg. She spent a week in the house before we managed to send her packing. From time to time wandering authors would turn up—bearded and long-skirted people, Talmudic philosophers, peddlers of their own printed aphorisms and dicta. They would leave us autographed copies and complain of being tormented by their evil wives. Once or twice in my life I was taken to a synagogue as if to a concert. There was a long wait to get in—one practically had to buy tickets from scalpers—and all that I saw and heard there caused me to return home in a heavy stupor. There is a Jewish quarter[11] in Petersburg: it begins just behind the Mariinskij Theater, where the ticket-scalpers freeze, beyond the prison angel of the Litovskij Castle, which was burned down in the Revolution. There on Torgovaja Street one sees Jewish shop-signs with pictures of a bull and a cow, women with an abundance of false hair showing under their kerchiefs, and, mincing along in overcoats reaching down to the ground, old men full of experience and philoprogeneity. The synagogue with its conical caps and onion domes loses itself like some elegant exotic fig tree amongst the shabby buildings. Velveteen berets with pom-poms, attendants and choristers on the point of physical exhaustion, clusters of seven-branched candelabra, tall vel-vet headdresses. The Jewish ship, with its sonorous alto choirs and the astonishing voices of its children, lays on all sail, split as it is by some ancient storm into male and female halves. Having blundered into the women's balcony, I edged along stealthily as a thief, hiding behind rafters. The Cantor, like Samson, collapsed the leonine building, he was answered by the velvet headdress, and the awe-some equilibrium of vowels and consonants in the im-peccably enunciated words imparted to the chants an in-vincible power. But how offensive was the crude speech of the rabbi—though it was not ungrammatical; how vulgar when he uttered the words "His Imperial Highness," how utterly vulgar all that he said! And all of a sudden two top-hatted gentlemen, splendidly dressed and glossy with wealth, with the refined movements of men of the world, touch the heavy book, step out of the circle and on behalf of everyone, with the authorization and commission of everyone, perform some honorary ritual, the principal thing in the ceremony. Who is that? Baron Ginzburg. And that? Varshavskij.

In my childhood I absolutely never heard Yiddish, only later did I hear an abundance of that melodious, always surprised and disappointed, interrogative language with its sharp accents on the weakly stressed syllables. The speech of the father and the speech of the mother—does not our language feed throughout all its long life on the confluence of these two, do they not compose its character? The speech of my mother was clear and sonorous without the least foreign admixture, with rather wide and too open vowels—the literary Great Russian language. Her vocabulary was poor and restricted, the locutions were trite, but it was a language, it had roots and confidence. Mother loved to speak and took joy in the roots and sounds of her Great Russian speech, impoverished by intellectual clichés. Was she not the first of her whole family to achieve pure and clear Russian sounds? My father had absolutely no language; his speech was tongue-tie and languagelessness. The Russian speech of a Polish Jew? No. The speech of a German Jew? No again. Perhaps a special Courland accent? I never heard such. A completely abstract, counterfeit language, the ornate and twisted speech of an autodidact, where normal words are intertwined with the ancient philosophical terms of Herder, Leibnitz, and Spinoza, the capricious syntax of a Talmudist, the artificial, not always finished sentence: it was anything in the world, but not a language, neither Russian nor German.

In essence, my father transferred me to a totally alien century and distant, although completely un-Jewish, atmosphere. These were, if you will, the purest eighteenth or even seventeenth century of an enlightened ghetto somewhere in Hamburg. Religious interests had been eliminated completely. The philosophy of the Enlightenment was transformed into intricate Talmudist pantheism. Somewhere in the vicinity Spinoza is breeding his spiders in a jar. One has a presentiment of Rousseau and his natural man. Everything fantastically abstract, intricate, and schematic. A fourteen-year-old boy, whom they had been training as a rabbi and had forbidden to read worldly books, runs off to Berlin and ends up in a higher Talmudic school, where there had gathered a number of such stubborn, rational youths, who had aspired in Godforsaken backwaters to be geniuses. Instead of the Talmud, he reads Schiller—and mark you, he reads it as a new book. Having held out here for a while, he falls out of this strange university back into the seething world of the seventies in order to remember the conspiratorial dairy shop on Karavannaja whence a bomb was tossed under Alexander, and in a glove-making shop and in a leather factory he expounds to the paunchy and astonished customers the philosophical ideals of the eighteenth century.

When I was taken to Riga, to my Riga grandparents, I resisted and nearly cried. It seemed to me that I was being taken to the native country of my father's incomprehensible philosophy. The artillery of band-boxes, baskets with padlocks, and all the chubby, awkward family baggage started upon its journey. The winter things were salted with coarse grains of naphthalene. The armchairs stood about like white horses in their stable bankets of slip covers. The preparations for the trip to the Riga coast seemed to me no fun. I used to collect nails at that time—the absurdest of collecting whimsies. I would run my hands through piles of nails like the Covetous Knight[12] and rejoice at the growth of my spiky wealth. Then they would take my nails away.

The trip was alarming. At night in Dorpat some sort of *Vereins* returning from a large songfest would storm the dimly lit carriage with their loud Estonian songs. The Estonians would stamp their feet and throw themselves through the door. It was very frightening.

My grandfather, a blue-eyed old man in a skull cap which covered half his forehead and with the serious and rather dignified features to be seen in very respected Jews, would smile, rejoice, and try to be affectionate—but did not know how. Then his dense eyebrows would draw together. When he wanted to take me in his arms I almost burst into tears. My kindly grandmother, wearing a black wig over her gray hair and a house coat with little yellow flowers, walked with tiny little steps over the creaking floorboards and was forever wanting people to eat something.

She kept asking, "Pokushali? Pokushali?" (Have you eaten?)—the only Russian word that she knew. But I did not like the old people's spicy dainties, with their bitter almond taste. My parents left to go to the city. My sombre grandfather and sad, bustling grandmother made an effort to distract me with conversation and ruffled their feathers like offended old birds. I tried to explain to them that I wanted to go to mama—they didn't understand. Then I represented my desire to leave by putting my index and middle figures through the motions of walking on the table.

Suddenly my grandfather drew from a drawer of a chest a black and yellow silk cloth, put it around my shoulders, and made me repeat after him words composed of unknown sounds; but, dissatisfied with my babble, he grew angry and shook his head in disapproval. I felt stifled and afraid. How my mother arrived just in time to save me I don't remember.

My father often spoke of my grandfather's honesty as of some lofty spiritual quality. For a Jew, honesty is wisdom and almost holiness. The farther one went back amongst the generations of these stern, blue-eyed old men, the more honesty and sternness one found. Great grandfather Veniamin once said, "I am closing down the business—I need no more money." He must have had just exactly enough to last him till the day of his death, since he did not leave a kopeck behind.

The Riga seaside is an entire country in itself. It is famed for its oozy, pure yellow, and astonishingly fine sand (even in an hour-glass one could hardly find such sand!) and also for the little boardwalks consisting of one or two hole-riddled planks that had been thrown down across the twenty versts of the villa-dotted Sahara.

There are no watering places anywhere that can compare with the swing and scope of the *dacha* life along the Riga coast. The boardwalks, flower beds, enclosed front gardens, and decorative glass balls stretch out in a huge, endless city, all on a yellow, finely milled, canary sand, such as children play with.

In the backyards Latvians dry and cure flounder, a one-eyed, bony fish, flat as a broad palm. The wailing of children, piano scales, the groans of patients from the innumerable dentists' offices, the clatter of crockery in the little resort pensions, the roulades of singers and the shouts of the peddlers—these noises are never silenced in the labyrinth of kitchen gardens, bakeries and barbed wire, and as far as the eye can see along the sand embankment run little toy trains, shod with rails and filled to overflowing with "hares"[13] who leap about during the trip from prim German Bilderlingshof to congested Jewish Dubbeln, which smelled of swaddling clothes.[14] Wandering musicians strolled about among the sparse pine groves: two convoluted trumpets, a clarinet and a trombone. Forever being chased away, they blow out their mercilessly false brass note and now here, now there, strike up the equestrian march of the splendid Karolina.

The whole region was controlled by a monocled baron named Firks. He divided his land into two parts: that which had been cleansed of Jews and that which had not. In the clean half, German students sat scraping their beer steins about on small tables. In the Jewish section babies' diapers hung from lines, and piano scales would gasp for breath. In the Germans' Majorenhof there were concerts: Strauss's *Death and Transfiguration* played by a symphony orchestra in the shell in the park. Elderly German women, their cheeks glowing and their mourning freshly donned, found it consoling.

In Jewish Dubbeln the orchestra strained at Tchaikovsky's *Symphonie Pathétique*, and one could hear the two nests of strings calling back and forth to each other.

At this time I conceived for Tchaikovsky a painfully nervous and tense love that recalled the desire of Dostoevsky's Netochka Nezvanova to hear the violin concerto behind the red flame of the silk curtains. The broad, flowing, purely violin passages in Tchaikovsky I heard from behind a barbed-wire fence and more than once tore my clothes and

covered my hands with scratches as I made my way gratis to
the orchestra shell. From the wild discordant gramophone
of music emanating from the *dachas* I would pick out the
strong violin passages. I do not remember how this venera-
tion of mine for the symphony orchestra was developed,
but I think that I correctly understood Tchaikovsky, having
guessed in him a special sense for the concertante.

What conviction sounded in those violin voices, softened
by Italian docility but still Russian, in the dirty Jewish
sewer! What a thread it is that runs from these first wretched
concerts to the silk flame of the Nobility Hall and frail
Scriabin, whom one expected to see crushed at any moment
by the still mute semicircle of singers about him and the
string forest of *Prometheus*, above which there hung like a
shield a sound recording device, a strange glass apparatus.[15]

· VII ·

The Concerts of Hofmann and Kubelik

In the season of 1903-04 Petersburg witnessed concerts in
the grand manner. I am speaking of the strange, never-to-
be-surpassed madness of the concerts of Hofmann and
Kubelik in the Nobility Hall during Lent.[16] I can recall
no other musical experiences, not even the première of
Scriabin's *Prometheus*, that might be compared with these
Lenten orgies in the white-columned hall. The concerts
would reach a kind of rage, a fury. This was no musical
dilettantism: there was something threatening and even
dangerous that rose up out of enormous depths, a kind of
craving for movement; a mute prehistorical malaise was
exuded by the peculiar, the almost flagellant zeal of the
guards in Mikhajlovskij Square, and it whetted the Peters-

burg of that day (the year 1905 had not yet struck) like a knife. In the dim light of the gas lamps the many entrances of the Nobility Hall were beset by a veritable siege. Gendarmes on prancing horses, lending to the atmosphere of the square the mood of a civil disturbance, made clicking noises with their tongues and shouted as they guarded the main entry with a chain. The sprung carriages with dim lanterns slipped into the glistening circle and arranged themselves in an impressive black gypsy camp. The cabbies dared not deliver their fares right to the door; one paid them while approaching, and then they made off rapidly to escape the wrath of the police. Through the triple chains the Petersburger made his way like a feverish little trout to the marble ice-hole of the vestibule, whence he disappeared into the luminous frosty building, bedraped with silk and velvet. The orchestra seats and the places behind those were filled in the customary order, but the spacious balconies to which the side entrances gave access were filled in bunches, like baskets with clusters of humanity. The Nobility Hall inside is wide, stocky, and almost square. The stage itself takes up very nearly half the area. The gallery swelters in a July heat. The air is filled with a ceaseless humming like that of cicadas over the steppe.

Who were Hofmann and Kubelik? To begin with, in the consciousness of the Petersburg populace of that time, they had become amalgamated into one image. Like twins, they were identical in height and in the color of their hair. Smaller than the average, almost dwarfish, they had hair blacker than a raven's wing. Both had a very low forehead and very small hands. As I recall them now, they both seem to have been something like leading men in some troupe of Lilliputians. I was taken to the Hôtel d'Europe[17] to pay my respects to Kubelik, although I did not play the violin. He lived like a real prince. Fearing that the boy might play the violin, he waved his little hand in alarm, but was immediately reassured and gave his autograph as he was requested to do.

Now when these two little musical demigods, these two *jeunes premiers* of the Lilliputian theater, had to make their way across the stage, sagging under the pressure of the crowd, I would be terrified for them. It would begin as with an electric spark, like the first gust of an approaching thunderstorm. Then the attendants would with difficulty clear a path through the throng, and to the accompaniment of an indescribable roar from all sides of the hot shoving human mass—neither bowing nor smiling, almost trembling, and with a kind of angry expression on their faces— they would make their way to the music stand and the piano. To this day that passage strikes me as perilous: I cannot get rid of the thought that the crowd, simply from not knowing what to do, was ready to tear its darlings to pieces. In what followed, these little geniuses, holding sway over the stunned musical mob of maids of honor and girl students, fat art patrons and shock-headed singing coaches, would try with all the means of their art, with all the logic and splendor of their sound, to chain and cool the unbridled Dionysian element. I have never heard from anyone such a pure, primordially clear, and transparent sound, in the piano sober as spring water, and producing in the violin a voice of the utmost simplicity, indivisible into its component filaments; and I have never again heard such a virtuoso, such an alpine cold, as in the frugality, sobriety, and formal clarity of these two legalists of the violin and the pianoforte. But what in their performance was clear and sober served only to enrage and incite to new frenzies the crowd that clung to the marble columns, hung in clusters from the gallery, sprouted from the flower-beds of the orchestra, and thickened hotly on the stage. Such was the power in the rational and pure playing of these two virtuosi.

The Tenishev School

On Zagorodnyj Prospekt, in the courtyard of a huge apartment house, one side of which was a blank wall that could be seen from a great distance and which bore an advertisement for Shustov cognac, about thirty boys dressed in shorts, wool socks, and English blouses played soccer to the accompaniment of horrendous shouting. They all looked as if they had been transported to England or Switzerland and there fitted out in a way that was not either Russian or that of a Gymnasium student, but somehow rather Cambridge in style.

I recall a solemn occasion: an unctuous priest in a violet cassock, the excited audience attending the opening day exercises, and suddenly all make way amidst a fluster of whispers: Witte had arrived.[18] It was commonly said of Witte that he had a golden nose, and the children, who blindly believed this, looked at nothing but his nose. The nose, however, was ordinary and appeared fleshy.

What was said then I do not remember; but on Mokhovaja Street in our own amphitheater, with its comfortable deputy's seats à la parliament there took place a rather elaborate ritual, and in the early days of September there would be formal exercises to celebrate the good fortune of our exemplary school. At these meetings, which resembled a juvenile House of Lords, an elderly doctor of hygiene named Virenius would inevitably say a few words. He was a rosy-cheeked old man, like the child on a can of Nestlé's. Every year he gave one and the same talk: on the beneficial effects of swimming. Since all this would take place in the fall, with the next swimming season about ten months away, there was something malapropos about his maneuvers and demonstrations, but this apostle of swimming regularly delivered his sermon every year on the very threshold of winter. Another hygienist was a professor named Prince Tarkhanov, an Oriental gentleman with an Assyrian beard, who used to go from desk to desk during the physiology lesson and make the students listen to his heart through his thick vest. One could not be sure whether it was a heart ticking or a gold watch, but the vest was indispensable.

The amphitheater with its collapsible desks, its capacious aisles dividing it into sections, and its strong overhead light, would be taken by storm on such grand occasions, and all Mokhovaja Street would seethe, inundated by the police and the massed intelligentsia.

This was all at the beginning of the 1900's.

The Tenishev auditorium was most often engaged by that citadel of radicalism the Literary Fund, which held the copyright on the works of Nadson. The Literary Fund was by its nature a commemorative organization: it revered. It had a meticulously worked out annual program, something like a calendar of saints, in accordance with which it celebrated the anniversaries of birth and death of, if I am not mistaken, Nekrasov, Nadson, Pleshcheev, Garshin, Turgenev, Gogol, Pushkin, Apukhtin, Nikitin, and others. These literary requiems were all alike, and in the choice of things to be read little attention was given to the question whether the deceased had actually written it.

It usually began with the aged Pëtr Isaevič Weinberg,[19] a kind of goat in a plaid lap robe, reading one invariable selection: "In front of me the sea, my old friend, unfolded like an endless shroud. . . ."

Then there would appear Samojlov, the actor from the Aleksandrinskij Theater, to read Nikitin's poem "The Master" in a heart-rending voice, striking himself on the breast and delivering himself of staggering shouts which subsided into sinister whispering.

Next would follow the conversation of the ladies, delightful in every respect, from *Dead Souls*. Then Nekrasov's "Grandfather Mazaj and the Hares" or "Reflections at the Main Entrance." Vedrinskaja would twitter Fet's poem "I come to you with greetings . . ." and the conclusion would be the playing of Chopin's *Funeral March*.

So much for literature. Now the performances of a civic nature. There were first of all the sessions of the Juridical Society, led by Maksim Kovalevskij and Petrunkevich,[20] where amidst a low hissing and buzzing they decanted the poison of constitutionalism. Maksim Kovalevskij, carrying all before him by virtue of his imposing figure, would preach an Oxfordian legality. While all about him heads were being chopped off, he delivered an immensely long and erudite speech on the right of perlustration, i.e., the censoring of private correspondence, in the course of which he cited the English example, admitted such a right, then qualified it, and finally curtailed it. The celebrants of these civic services were M. Kovalevskij, Rodichev, Nikolaj Fëdorovich Annenskij, Batjushkov, and Ovsjaniko-Kulikov-skij.[21]

It was in the near proximity of such a domestic forum as this that we received our education in the high glass boxes with steam-heated windowsills which were our huge class-rooms, seating 25 students. And our corridors were not corridors but riding halls with tall ceilings and parqueted floors, the atmosphere of which, crossed by slanting columns of dust-laden sunlight, generally smelled of gas from the physics laboratories. The practical demonstrations consisted of cruel and needless vivisections, the expulsion of all the air from a glass bell in order to observe a poor mouse die of suffocation on its back, the torturing of frogs, the scientific boiling of water, with a description of this process, and the melting of little glass rods on the gas burners.

The heavy, sweetish smell of gas in the laboratories gave one a headache, but the real hell for the majority of the awkward, nervous, and not unduly healthy children was the class of manual crafts. Towards the end of the day, heavy with lessons and sated with conversations and demonstrations, we would gasp with fatigue among the wood shavings and sawdust, unable to saw a board in half. The saw would get bent, the plane would go crooked, the chisel would strike against fingers: nothing came out right. The instructor would busy himself with two or three of the skillful boys, and the others would damn all handicrafts.

At our German lessons we would sing "O Tannenbaum, O Tannenbaum!" under the direction of the Fräulein, who also used to bring to class pictures of milky alpine landscapes with dairy cows and little tile-roofed houses.

There was in the school a military, privileged, almost aristocratic undercurrent that was forever threatening to break through: this was composed of the children of certain ruling families who had landed here by some strange parental caprice and now lorded it over the flabby intellectuals.[22] A certain Voevodskij, the son of a court official and a strikingly handsome boy with a classical profile in the style of Nicholas I, proclaimed himself "commander" and compelled everyone to take an oath of fealty to him, kissing the cross and Bible.

Here is a short portrait gallery of my class.

Vanjusha Korsakov. Nicknamed "Porkchop." Flaccid boy from a family with ties to the *zemstvo* tradition (Petrunkevich, Rodichev). Wore his hair in a bowl cut. A Russian shirt with a silk belt.

Barats. His family intimate with Stasjulevich[23] (*Messenger of Europe*). A passionate mineralogist, mute as a fish, talks only of quartz and mica.

Leonid Zarubin. Large coal-mining industry in the Don Basin. To begin with, dynamos and batteries; later on, nothing but Wagner.

Przesiecki. Poor Polish gentry. Specialist at spitting.

Słobodzinski. Top student. A person from the second part of *Dead Souls*, burned by Gogol. Positive type of the

Russian *intelligent*. Moderate mystic. Truth lover. Good mathematician. Well read in Dostoevsky. Later on he ran a radio station.

Nadezhdin. A classless intellectual. Sour odor from the apartment of a minor clerk. Gaiety and insouciance, since there was nothing to lose.

The Krupenskijs. Twins. Landed gentry from Bessarabia. Connoisseurs of wine and Jews.

And finally, Boris Sinani. Belonged to the generation that is now active, having ripened for great events and historical work. He had hardly graduated before he died. How he would have shone during the years of the revolution!

There are still today various old ladies and good provincial people who, when they wish to praise someone, say that he is "a luminous personality."[24] And I understand what they mean. There is no other way to speak of our Ostrogorskij except in the language of that period, and the old-fashioned pompousness of that absurd expression no longer strikes one as comical. It was only during the first few years of the century that the coattails of Ostrogorskij could be seen flitting about the corridors of the Tenishev School. He was near-sighted and squinted, his eyes brilliant with mockery—a great, scrofulous ape in a frock coat, with a beard and hair of golden-red. There was, I am sure, something very Chekhovian about his incredible smile. He did not take root, somehow, in the twentieth century, though he wanted to. He loved Blok (and at what an early date!), and published his poems in his journal *Education*.

He was no administrator—he just squinted and smiled and was terribly absentminded. It was rare to have a talk with him. He shrugged everything off with a joke, even when there was no call to do so.

"What class do you have now?"

"Geology."

"Geology yourself."

The whole school, with all its humanistic twaddle and nonsense, was held together by his smile.

Still, there were some good boys in the Tenishev School. The same flesh and blood as the children in the portraits of Serov. Little ascetics, monks in their children's monastery, where the notebooks, equipment, glass retorts, and German books contained more spirituality and inner harmony than can be found in the grown-up world.

· IX ·

Sergej Ivanych

The year 1905 was the chimera of the Russian Revolution with the little lynx eyes of a policeman and wearing a student's blue beret, flat as a pancake! The Petersburgers could sense your coming from a great distance, they could catch the sound of your horses' hooves, and they shivered in your drafts in the alcohol-preserved auditoriums of the Military Medical College or in the immensely long *jeu de paume* of the Men'shikov University, where the future orator of the Armenians would roar like an enraged lion at some feeble SR or SD,[25] and those whose job it was to listen would stretch out their avine necks. Memory loves to go hunting in the dark, and it was in the densest possible murk that you were born, O moment, when—one, two, three—the Nevskij blinked shut its long electric lashes to bury itself in the blackness of outer night and from the far end of the boulevard there appeared out of the dense shaggy dark the chimera with its little lynx policeman eyes and flattened student's cap.

For me the year 1905 is in Sergej Ivanych. There were many of them—the tutors of the revolution! One of my friends, a rather haughty person, used to say, not without some justice, "Some men are books, others—newspapers." Poor Sergej Ivanych would not have found a place in such an analysis; for him it would have been necessary to establish a third category: some men are interlinear translations. Interlinear translations of the revolution poured from him, in his cold-stuffed head their cigarette-paper pages rustled, he shook from the cuffs of his sea-green cavalry jacket an ethereally light contraband literature, his Russian cigarette burned with a forbidden smoke, as if it had been rolled out of illegal paper.

I do not know where and how Sergej Ivanych had learned his trade. I was too young to know anything about that side of his life. But once he took me along to his place and I saw the room which served him for study, bedroom, and laboratory. At that time he and I were engaged in a large and grandly futile enterprise: writing a paper on the reasons for the fall of the Roman Empire. In the space of one week Sergej Ivanych dictated to me in sudden volleys 135 tightly crammed notebook pages. He would speak without a moment's reflection, without checking any sources, and like a spider would spin—out of cigarette smoke, I suppose—a fragile web of learned phraseology, drawing out lengthy periods and making little knots of the social and economic features. He enjoyed the patronage of our house, as of many others. Was this not the way Romans hired Greek slaves, so as to be able to shine at dinner by showing off some learned treatise? At the height of the work which I mentioned above Sergej Ivanych took me to his place. He lived somewhere in the 100 block of the Nevskij Prospekt, beyond the Nicholas Station, where all the houses have renounced any effort towards chic and are, like cats, gray. I shuddered at the heavy, acrid smell of Sergej Ivanych's dwelling. The atmosphere of the room, having been breathed and smoked for years, was by this time no longer air but some new and unknown substance with a different specific weight and other chemical properties. And I involuntarily recalled the dog cave of Naples from my physics course. During all the time that he had lived here the master of these quarters had never lifted or changed the position of anything and treated the arrangement of things like a veritable dervish, throwing permanently onto the floor whatever proved to be superfluous. At home, Sergej Ivanych recognized only the supine position. While he dictated, I would steal side glances at his coal-dust colored linen, and how astonished I was when Sergej Ivanych called a break and prepared two glasses of the most magnificent, thick, and aromatic hot chocolate. It turned out that he had a passion for chocolate. He cooked it with a master's touch—much stronger than the usual. What conclusion is one to draw from this? Was Sergej Ivanych a sybaritic voluptuary, or had some chocolate demon entered his soul, fastening itself upon this ascetic and nihilist? O, the gloomy authority of Sergej Ivanych, O, his subversive depths, his cavalry jacket and trousers of some gendarme material! His walk resembled that of a man who had just been seized by the shoulder and led into the presence of some terrible satrap while trying to appear completely nonchalant. It was an unadulterated pleasure to walk down the street with him, for he would point out all the government spies, of whom he was not in the least afraid.

I think that he was himself something like a spy—perhaps from his constant preoccupation with that subject, or perhaps from the law of protective coloration, which causes birds and butterflies to take their color and plumage from that of the cliff. Yes, there was in Sergej Ivanych something of the gendarme. He was querulous, he was peevish, he would wheeze the kind of anecdotes that generals like, and would utter the first five grades of the military and civil services with both relish and disgust. The sleepy face of Sergej Ivanych, crumpled like a student beret, always wore the expression of a purely gendarme disgust. To push some general or some Actual State Councilor face first into the mud was for him the very summit of happiness—a happiness, I think, rather mathematical and abstract.

Thus an anecdote in his mouth sounded like a theorem. A general runs through all the dishes on a menu, rejects them all, and exclaims: "What filth!" A student who had overheard the general's remark asks him to name the various ranks of the government service and when he has finished, exclaims: "Is that all? What filth!"

Somewhere in Siedlce or in Rovno, Sergej Ivanych, being at the time probably a boy of tender years, had broken away from some official police rock. His family tree included minor provincial governors of the Western Region, and he himself—this was after he had already become a tutor of the revolution and a slave to the chocolate demon—sought to marry some governor's daughter who had also, apparently, broken away for good. Of course, Sergej Ivanych was not a revolutionary. Let his epithet stick: a tutor of the revolution. Like a chimera he dissolved at the first light of the historic day. As the year 1905 and the fatal hour drew closer, his secrecy thickened and his gloomy authority increased. He should have shown himself at last, he should have taken some kind of decisive action, should have at least—well—brandished a revolver from the midst of an armed squad or given some other concrete proof of his consecration to the revolution.

But then, at the very height of the alarm in 1905, Sergej Ivanych became the guardian of the pleasantly and harmlessly frightened burghers, and, grinning with satisfaction like a cat, he brought reliable news that on such and such a day there would inevitably occur a pogrom of the Petersburg intelligentsia. As a member of one of the armed squads he promised to come with his Browning, guaranteeing everyone's complete safety.

I chanced to meet him many years after 1905. He was totally faded. He had absolutely no face, so erased and bleached were his features. A faint shadow of his former disgust and authority. It turned out that he had found a place and served as an assistant in the astronomical observatory at Pulkovo.

If Sergej Ivanych had been transformed into a pure logarithm of stellar velocities or a function of space it would not have surprised me. He had to depart this life, such a chimera was he.

....

· X ·

Julij Matveich

....

In the time it took Julij Matveich to climb up to the fifth floor one could have run down to the doorman and back several times. He had to be supported under the arms and allowed to stop for breath at each landing. In the entrance hall he would stop and wait while they took off his fur coat. A little man with short legs, wearing an old man's fur coat that reached to his heels and a heavy fur cap, he would puff and wheeze until he had been freed from the hot beaver fur, and then he would sit down on the divan with his legs sticking out like a child's. His appearance in the house signalled either a family council or the pacification of some domestic row. Every family is, when all is said and done, a government. He loved family fallings-out the way a government official loves political difficulties. He had no family of his own and had chosen to work on ours as being extraordinarily difficult and complex.

We children were seized by stormy joy the moment we caught sight of his ministerial head (so much like Bismarck's that it was funny), tender and bald as a baby's, not counting the three hairs on the very top.

In answer to a question Julij Matveich would make some indistinct sound with a strange chesty timbre, like something produced on a trumpet by an unskillful musician, and only after having made this preliminary noise would he commence his statement with the invariable phrase: "Didn't I tell you . . ." or "I always told you. . . ."

Childless, helplessly walrus-footed, the Bismarck of someone else's family, Julij Matveich inspired in me a profound sympathy.

He had grown up amongst enterprising southern landowners, somewhere between Bessarabia, Odessa, and Rostov.

How many contracts had been fulfilled, how many vineyard estates and stud farms sold with the aid of a Greek notary in the lousy hotel rooms of Kishinëv and Rostov! All of them—the Greek notary, the sharp-dealing landowner, and the gubernia secretary, a Moldavian—put on their white dusters and, in the choleraic heat, jolted along the highways and paved roads of the gubernia in a canopied *brichka*. It was there that his experience had multiplied and his capital rounded out, and together with this grew his epicureanism. His little arms and legs had already begun to refuse their function and were turning into short little flippers, and Julij Matveich, dining with the marshal of nobility and a contractor in the hotels of Kishinëv and Rostov, would summon the waiter with that same indistinct trumpet sound which I mentioned above. He was gradually transformed into a real Jewish general. Cast in iron, he might have served as a monument—but where and when could iron give a true notion of the three Bismarckian hairs? The world view of Julij Matveich grew to be something wise and cogent. His favorite reading was Men'shikov and Renan. A strange combination at first glance, but, when one thinks of it, even for a member of the government council it would have been impossible to choose better reading. About Men'shikov he said, raising his little senatorial hand, that he had an "intelligent head,"

and as for Renan, he agreed with him in absolutely everything concerning Christianity. Julij Matveich was con-
temptuous of death, hated doctors, and, as an edifying
instance, loved to tell of how he had escaped unharmed
from the cholera. In his youth he had made a trip to Paris,
and when, thirty years after the first trip, he found himself once more in Paris he refused to enter a single restaurant and kept looking for some "Coq d'or" where he had
once had a good meal. But the Coq d'or no longer existed.
A "Coq" did turn up, but it was the wrong one, and even
that was practically impossible to locate. Julij Matveich
went about the business of choosing dishes from the menu
with the air of a gourmet, the *garçon* was breathless in
anticipation of some complicated and subtle order, and then
Julij Matveich would settle on a cup of bouillon. It was no
easy matter to get ten or fifteen rubles out of Julij Matveich: He would expatiate for over an hour on sagacity,
epicureanism, and—"Didn't I tell you." Then he would
shuffle about the room for a long time looking for the keys,
wheeze, and root about in concealed drawers.

The death of Julij Matveich was terrible. He died like
the old man in Balzac, practically thrown out on the street
by a shrewd and powerful family of shopkeepers, to whom
he had in his old age transferred his services as a domestic
Bismarck and whom he had permitted to take over his
life.

They drove the dying Julij Matveich out of their commercial quarters on Razezzhaja Street and rented a room
for him in a small *dacha* in the Lesnoj section.

Unshaven and in a frightful condition, he sat with his
spittoon and a copy of the *New Times*. His deadly blue
cheeks were covered with a dirty bristle. In his trembling
hand he held a magnifying glass and moved it along the
lines of the paper. In the dark pupils of his eyes, afflicted
with cataract, there lay the fear of death. The servant would

place a dish before him and immediately disappear without asking whether he needed anything.

To the funeral of Julij Matveich there came an extraordinary number of relatives, respectable and unknown to each other, and his nephew from the Azov-Don Bank shuffled about on his little short legs and kept shaking his heavy Bismarckian head.

....

· XI ·

The Erfurt Program

....

"Why do you read pamphlets? What kind of sense is there in them?"—the voice of the extremely intelligent V.V.G.[26] sounds right above my ear. "You want to learn something about Marxism? Get Marx's *Kapital*." So I got it, got burnt by it, and threw it away: back again to the pamphlets. Och . . . wasn't my splendid Tenishev mentor playing a trick on me? Marx's *Kapital* is the same as Kraevich's *Physics*. Surely no one can think that Kraevich leads to any new ideas. But a pamphlet plants a little larva— that is just its function. And the larva gives birth to thought.

What a hodgepodge, what true historical dissonance lived in our school, where geography, puffing away at a pipeful of "Capstan" tobacco, was transformed into anecdotes about American trusts, what a lot of history knocked and fluttered alongside the Tenishev hothouse on its chicken legs[27] and beside the troglodytic soccer games.

No, Russian boys are not English. You won't catch them with sport or with the boiled water of political amateurism. Life, with all its unexpected interests and its passionate intellectual diversions, life will burst in upon the most hothouse-like, the most completely sterilized Russian school, as it once burst into Pushkin's lycée.

A copy of *The Scales* under the desk, and next to it the slag and metal shavings from the Obukhov factory, and not a word, not a sound, as though by some conspiracy, about Belinskij, Dobroljubov, or Pisarev; Bal'mont, however, was held in high regard and his imitators weren't bad; and the Social Democrat is at the throat of the Populist, drinking his SR blood, and the latter calls in vain upon the princes of his church—Chernov, Mikhajlovskij, and even— the *Historical Letters* of Lavrov.[28] Everything that represented an attitude toward life was greedily devoured. I repeat: my schoolmates could not endure Belinskij on account of the diffuseness of his attitude toward life, but Kautsky was respected, and so was Protopop Avvakum, whose autobiography, in the Pavlenkov edition, was made a part of our study of Russian literature.

Of course, none of this could have been without V.V.G., the moulder of souls and teacher for remarkable people (only it turned out that there were none on hand). But about him more later; for now, hail and farewell to Kautsky, the thin red band of light in the east of the Marxist dawn!

Early, O Erfurt Program, you Marxist propylaea, too early did you train our spirits to a sense of harmoniousness, but to me and to many others you gave a sense of life in those prehistoric years when thought hungered after unity and harmoniousness, when the backbone of the age was becoming erect, when the heart needed more than anything the red blood of the aorta! Is Kautsky Tjutchev? Surely he was not gifted with the power to evoke cosmic sensations ("And the thin thread of the spider's web trembles on the empty furrow.")? But just imagine—for a person at a certain age and at a certain moment Kautsky (I say Kautsky, of course, just as an example and might with even greater justice have said Marx, Plekhanov) *is* Tjutchev, that is, the source of a cosmic joy, the bearer of a strong and harmonious attitude toward life, the thinking reed, and a cover thrown over the abyss.

That year, in Segewold, on the Courland river Aa, there was a radiant autumn with spider webs in the fields of barley. The estates of the barons had just been burned down, and after the pacification there arose out of the charred brick outbuildings a grim cruel silence. From time to time there would come clattering along the hard German road a two-wheeled cart with the bailiff and a constable and some oaf of a Latvian would doff his cap. In its brick-red, layered, cave-riddled banks the romantic little river flowed along like a German water nymph and the towns were sunk up to their ears in green foliage. The inhabitants kept a dim memory of Konevskoj,[29] who had recently drowned in the river. That was a young man who had reached maturity too early and was thus not read by Russian youth: his lines had a difficult sound like the rustling of the roots of a forest. And so, in Segewold with the Erfurt Program in my hands, I was closer in spirit to Konevskoj than if I had poeticized à la Zhukovskij and the Romantics, because I was able to populate, to socialize the visible world with its barley, dirt roads, castles, and sunlit spider webs, breaking it down into diagrams and setting up under the pale blue firmament ladders, far from biblical, upon which not the angels of Jacob but small and large property holders ascended and descended, passing through the stages of capitalist economy.

What could be stronger, what could be more organic: I perceived the entire world as an economy, a human economy—and the shuttles of English domestic industry that had fallen silent a hundred years ago sounded once more in the ringing autumn air! Yes, I heard with the sharpness of ears caught by the sound of a distant threshing machine in the field the burgeoning and increase, not of the barley in its ear, not of the northern apple, but of the world, the capitalist world, that was ripening in order to fall!

The Sinani Family

When I arrived in class a completely prepared and finished Marxist, I was awaited by a very serious opponent. When he had listened intently to my self-assured speeches, there came up to me a boy wearing a thin belt around his waist, his hair almost red, and somehow narrow all over— narrow in the shoulders, with a narrow face, gentle and manly, narrow hands, and little feet. Above his lip he had a red splotch, like a fiery sign. There was little in his dress to recall the Anglo-Saxon style of the Tenishev School. It was as if they had taken an old, old pair of trousers and a shirt, scrubbed them very hard with soap in a cold stream, dried them in the sun, and given them to him, unironed, to put on. Anyone looking at him would have said, What frail bones! But anyone glancing at his high, modest forehead would have been astonished at his almost slanted eyes, which had a greenish cast to their smile, and would have been stopped by the expression of his small mouth, bitterly proud. His movements, when necessary, could be large and bold, like the gesture of the boy playing jacks in Fëdor Tolstoy's sculpture, but he generally avoided sharp movements, saving his accuracy and lightness for play. His walk was astonishingly light—a barefoot walk. It would have suited him to have a sheep dog at his legs and a long staff in his hands. His cheeks and chin were covered with a golden, animal down. He was something between a Russian boy playing a Russian game and an Italian John the Baptist with a barely noticeable hook in his sharp nose.

He volunteered to be my teacher, and I did not leave him for as long as he lived, but followed after him, rapt by the clarity of his mind, by his courage, by the presence of his spirit. He died on the eve of the arrival of the historic days for which he had prepared himself, for which nature had prepared him, just at the moment when the sheepdog was ready to lie down calmly at his feet and the slender staff of the Baptist was to have been exchanged for the rod of the shepherd. His name was Boris Sinani. I utter that name with tenderness and respect. He was the son of the famous Petersburg doctor who treated people by means of suggestion, Boris Naumovich Sinani. His mother was Russian, but his father stemmed from the Karaite Jews of the Crimea. Could this not account for the duality of his appearance? A Russian boy from Novgorod, but with an un-Russian aquiline nose and on his skin the golden down of a Crimean shepherd from the Yaila Mountains. From the earliest moment of his conscious existence Boris Sinani, by a tradition of his strong and extraordinarily interesting family, regarded himself as the chosen vessel of Russian Populism. It seems to me that what attracted him in Populism was not its theory but rather the quality of its spirit. One felt in him a realist ready to abandon all arguments, when necessary, for the sake of action, but for the time being his youthful realism, free of anything that was trivial and deadening, was charming and breathed with an innate spirituality and nobility. With a deft hand Boris Sinani removed from my eyes the cataract which, he believed, had prevented my seeing the agrarian question. The Sinanis lived on Pushkin Street, opposite the hotel Palais Royal. They were a powerful family in the strength of their intellectual character, which sometimes took the form of an eloquent primitiveness. Dr. Boris Naumovich Sinani had evidently lived on Pushkin Street for a long time. The gray-haired doorman had a boundless respect for the entire family, from the ferocious psychiatrist Boris Naumovich all the way to the little hunchback Lenochka. No one crossed that threshold without trepidation, since Boris Naumovich reserved the right to eject anyone to whom he took a dislike, whether it was a patient or simply a guest who had said something stupid. Boris Naumovich Sinani was the physician and executor of Gleb Uspenskij, the friend of Nikolaj Konstantinovich Mikhajlovskij—by whose personality, incidentally, he was far from being always blinded—and the advisor and confidant of the leading SR's of that day.

His appearance was that of a stocky Karaite Jew—he even kept the Karaite cap—with a hard and unusually heavy face. Not everyone could endure the savage, intelligent gaze through his eyeglasses; when he smiled, though, into his curly, sparse beard, his smile was that of a child and altogether charming. Entrance into the study of Boris Naumovich was strictly forbidden. There, by the way, hung his emblem and the emblem of the whole house, the portrait of Shchedrin, glowering from beneath his dense gubernatorial brows and menacing the children with the frightful spade of his shaggy beard. This Shchedrin looked like something between the demon in Gogol's *Vij* and a governor, and he was terrifying, especially in the dark. Boris Naumovich was a widower, and about his widowerhood there was something stubborn and wolfish. He lived with his son and two daughters, Zhenja, the elder, slant-eyed as a Japanese and very miniature and elegant, and the little hunchback Lena. He had few patients, but those whom he had he held in servile terror, especially the women. In spite of the rudeness of his manner, they would present him with little embroidered shoes and slippers. In his leather study under the beard of Shchedrin he lived like a forester in his lodge, and on all sides he was surrounded by enemies: mysticism, stupidity, hysteria, and boorishness. If you must live with wolves, then howl like a wolf.

Even among the most outstanding men of that time the authority of Mikhajlovskij was obviously enormous, and it is not likely that Boris Naumovich found this easy to accept. By virtue of some fatal contradiction, he himself,

an ardent rationalist, needed authority and revered authority and this tortured him. Whenever some abrupt changes
occurred unexpectedly in the political or social sphere,
the question was instantly raised in the house, What would
Nikolaj Konstantinovich say? In a short while the senate
of the Populist journal *Russian Wealth* would actually be
called into session at Mikhajlovskij's and Nikolaj Konstantinovich would deliver himself of his opinions. It was
precisely these pronouncements that the elder Sinani valued
in Mikhajlovskij. The scale of his reverence for the leaders
of Populism was constituted thus: Mikhajlovskij was good
as an oracle, but his journalistic writing was pure water,
and as a man he was not respectable. When all was said
and done, he did not like Mikhajlovskij. He conceded that
Chernov had gumption and a peasant, agrarian intellect.
Peshekhonov he regarded as a dishcloth. He felt some tenderness for Mjakotin as the Benjamin of the lot. Not one
of them did he take seriously. He genuinely respected the
elderly Natanson, a member of the central committee of
the SR party.[30] Gray, bald, looking like an old doctor,
Natanson came to the house two or three times to talk with
Boris Naumovich, and his visits were not kept secret from
us children. There was no limit to the excited flutter and
proud joy: the house contained a member of the Central
Committee.

The domestic order of the house, in spite of its lack of
a mistress, was strict and simple, as in the family of a merchant. The little hunchbacked girl Lena very nearly ran
the house, but such was the harmony of the will which
ruled here that the house kept itself.

I knew what Boris Naumovich was doing in his study.
He kept reading and reading harmful, foolish books filled
with mysticism, hysteria, and all manner of pathology; he
struggled with them, he settled accounts with them, but he
could not tear himself away from them and kept forever
coming back to them. Set him a diet of pure positivism and

old Sinani would have immediately shriveled up. Positivism is good for a shareholder, it brings in its five per cent of progress annually. Boris Naumovich required sacrifices for the glory of positivism. He was the Abraham of positivism, and would not have hesitated to sacrifice his own son to it.

Once, at tea, there was a mention of life after death, and Boris Naumovich raised his eyes in astonishment. "What is that? Do I remember what was before my birth? I remember nothing. There was nothing. And after death there won't be anything."

His Bazarovism had finally a classical Greek simplicity. Even the one-eyed cook became infected with the general atmosphere.

The central feature of the Sinani household was what I should call an aesthetic of the intellect. Positivism is usually hostile to aesthetic contemplation, the disinterested pride and joy of the movements of the mind. But for these people the intellect was joy, health, sport, and almost religion, all at once. The circle of their intellectual interests was, however, extremely limited, their field of vision was narrow, and the fact is that their avid minds had to gnaw on scanty nourishment: the eternal quarrels of the SR's and SD's, the role of personality in history, the notorious harmonious personality of Mikhajlovskij, the agrarian badgering of the SD's—that was the poor extent of it. Bored by the thought he found at home, Boris lost himself in reading the legal speeches of Lassalle—marvelously constructed, fascinating and full of life. That was in truth pure intellectual aesthetics and real sport. And in imitating Lassalle we were carried away by the sport of eloquence, oratorical improvisation. Much in vogue were agrarian philippics directed against an assumed target from among the SD's. Some of these speeches offered to the void were positively brilliant. I still recall how at one meeting Boris, still a boy at the time, hounded an experienced old Menshevik named Kleinbort,[31] a contributor to the learned quarterlies, and

caused him to break into a sweat. Kleinbort simply panted
and looked around in confusion: the mental elegance of his
opponent apparently struck him as a new and unexpected
weapon of argument. All this, to be sure, was nothing
more than the pebbles that Demosthenes carried about in
his mouth, but God save any youthful orators from such
teachers as N. K. Mikhajlovskij! What a windbag that
was! What Manilovism!! Dressed out with truisms and
arithmetical computations, that empty blather about the
harmonious personality crept out like a weed from everywhere and occupied the place of living, fruitful thought.

According to the constitution of the house the heavy old
man Sinani dared not so much as glance into the young
people's room, called the pink room. The pink room cor-
responded to the divan room in *War and Peace*. Of the
visitors to the pink room, of whom there were not many,
I recall one, a certain Natasha, a nice, nonsensical creature.
Boris Naumovich tolerated her as a kind of household fool.
Natasha was in turn an SD, an SR, a Russian Orthodox,
a Roman Catholic, a Hellenist, and a Theosophist, with
various intermissions for breath. This frequent change of
her convictions caused her to turn prematurely gray. While
she was a Hellenist she published a novel based on the life
of Julius Caesar at the Roman spa in Baiae, Baiae having
assumed a striking resemblance to Sestroretsk (Natasha was
terribly wealthy).

In the pink room as in every divan room confusion
reigned. And what constituted the confusion that reigned
in the aforesaid divan room at the beginning of this current century? Wretched postcards with allegories of Stuck
and Zhukov,[32] the "fairytale postcard" (something straight
out of Nadson), bareheaded and with twisted arms, a char-
coal enlargement printed on an oversized card. The terrible publication called *The Reader and Declaimer*, and
all sorts of *Russian Muses* with P. Ja., Mikhajlov, and
Tarasov,[33] where we made a conscientious search for poetry

but were, anyway, sometimes embarrassed. Much attention was devoted to Mark Twain and Jerome K. Jerome (the best and most wholesome of all our reading). A rubbish heap of various *Anathemas, Sweetbriers,* and the miscellanies put out by the Znanie publishing house. Our evenings were grounded in the vague recollections of the estate in Luga where the guests would sleep on the little semi-circular sofas in the parlor and the six poor aunts would all run everything at once. Then there were diaries and autobiographical novels in the bargain: was there not enough confusion?

One person who was practically a member of the family in the Sinani house was Semën Akimych Anskij, who would drop out of sight occasionally on some Jewish business in Mogilëv and then turn up again in Petersburg to spend the night beneath Shchedrin, though without the right of domicile. Semën Akimych Anskij combined in himself a Jewish folklorist with Gleb Uspenskij and Chekhov. In his single person he contained a thousand provincial rabbis, if one reckons by the amount of his advice and consolations, conveyed in the guise of parables, anecdotes, and so on. All that Semën Akimych needed in life was a place to spend the night and strong tea. People ran after him to hear his stories. The Russian-Jewish folklore of Semën Akimych flowed out like a thick stream of honey in marvelous unhurried stories. Semën Akimych was not yet old but he had an aged grandfatherly appearance and was stooped over from the excess of Jewishness and Populism: governors, pogroms, human misfortunes, encounters, the most cunning patterns of public life in the improbable circumstances of the Minsk and Mogilëv satrapies, etched as though with a fine engraving needle. Semën Akimych preserved everything, remembered everything—a Gleb Uspenskij out of the Talmud-Torah. Behind the modest tea table he sat with his gentle biblical gestures, his head inclined to one side, like the Jewish apostle Peter at the Last

Supper. In a house where everyone was knocking against the graven image of Mikhajlovskij and cracking the tough agrarian nut, Semën Akimych gave the impression of a gentle hemorrhoidal Psyche.

At that time modernism and symbolism somehow managed to live together in my head with the most desperate Nadsonism and the poesy from the journal *Russian Wealth*. I had already read all of Blok, including *The Puppet Show*, and he got on splendidly with the civic themes and all that gibberish verse. He was not ill disposed toward it; in fact, it was from there that he himself issued. The "thick reviews"[34] bred a kind of poetry to wilt the ears, and it was there that the most attractive little loopholes were kept for the eccentric failures, young suicides, and poetic underground men, who differed little from the homey lyricists of *Russian Wealth* and *The Messenger of Europe*.

On Pushkin Street, in a very decent apartment, there lived a former German banker by the name of Goldberg, the editor and publisher of a little magazine called *The Poet*.

Goldberg, a fat bourgeois, considered himself a German poet, and he entered into the following agreement with his clients: he would print their verses gratis in the magazine *Poet*, and in return they would undertake to listen to his, Goldberg's, composition, a lengthy German philosophical poem with the title *The Parliament of the Insects*—in German, or in the case of someone's not knowing German, then in Russian translation.

To all his clients Goldberg would say, "Young man, your writing is going to become better and better."[35] He especially prized one gloomy poet whom he considered to have suicidal tendencies. Goldberg had hired a youth of the most heavenly poetic appearance to help him put the issues together. The old chronic failure of a banker and his Schilleresque assistant—who was, by the way, the translator of the *Parliament of Insects* into Russian—labored selflessly over that dear misshapen magazine. Some strange banker's muse guided the pudgy fingers of Goldberg. The Schiller in his employ was evidently pulling his leg. In Germany, though, when times were good, Goldberg had printed a collected edition of his works, which he himself showed to me.

How profoundly Boris Sinani understood the essence of the Socialist Revolutionary doctrine and how far, even as a boy, he had spiritually outgrown it can be seen in a nickname which he invented; we used to call a certain type of person of the SR persuasion "Christlings"—very wicked irony, you must admit. The "Christlings" were those infinitely Russian people with gentle faces, the bearers of "the idea of personality in history," who in fact, many of them, really did look like Nesterov's paintings of Jesus. Women were very fond of them, and they themselves were easily enflamed. At the polytechnical balls held in the Lesnoj quarter such a "Christling" would serve as a Childe Harold, an Onegin, or a Pechorin. In general, the revolutionary rabble of the days of my youth, the innocent "periphery," seethed with novels. In 1905, boys went into the revolution with the same feelings as Nikolen'ka Rostov had on going into the Hussars: it was a question of love and honor. To both, life seemed impossible unless it were warmed by the glory of one's age; both thought it impossible to breathe without valor. *War and Peace* lived on—only the glory had moved elsewhere. Glory was not, after all, with Colonel Min of the Semënovskij Regiment and it was not with the generals in polished boots who rode in the Emperor's retinue. Glory was in the Central Committee, glory was in the "fighting organization,"[36] and feats of valor began with a novitiate as a propagandist.

Late autumn in Finland, a remote *dacha* in Raivola. Everything boarded up, the wickets barred, the wolfhounds snarling beside empty summer houses. Fall overcoats and old lap robes. The warmth of a kerosene lamp on a cold balcony. The fox snout of young T., living in the reflected glory of his father, a member of the Central Committee. No mistress of the house, but a timid consumptive creature who was not even allowed to look the guests in the face. One by one out of the darkness of the *dachas* they approach in English greatcoats and bowler hats. Sit quietly, do not go upstairs. Passing through the kitchen, one noticed the large, closely cropped head of Gershuni.[37]

War and Peace goes on. The wet wings of glory strike at the window: both ambition and the same craving for honor! The midnight sun in a Finland blind with rain, the conspiratorial sun of the new Austerlitz! Boris, dying, had hallucinations of Finland and raved of the move to Raivola and of some sort of cords for packing the baggage. We used to play skittles here, and Boris, lying in a Finnish meadow, loved to gaze into the blank sky with the cold astonished eyes of Prince Andrew.

I was troubled and anxious. All the agitation of the times communicated itself to me. There were strange currents loosed about me—from the longing for suicide to the expectation of the end of the world. The literature of problems and ignorant universal questions had just taken its gloomy malodorous leave, and the grimy hairy hands of the traffickers in life and death were rendering the very words life and death repugnant. That was in very truth the night of ignorance! Literati in Russian blouses and black shirts traded, like grain dealers, in God and the Devil, and there was not a single house where the dull polka from *The Life of Man*, which had become a symbol of vulgar tawdry symbolism, was not picked out with one finger on the piano. For too long the intelligentsia had been fed on student songs. Now it was repelled by its universal questions. The same philosophy from a beer bottle!

That was all the vilest scum when compared to the world of the Erfurt Program, the Communist Manifestoes, and agrarian debates. They had their own Protopop Avvakum and their own dispute over whether the sign of the cross was to be made with two fingers or three (for example, the question of horseless peasants). Here in the deep and passionate strife of the SR's and SD's one could sense the continuation of the ancient feud of the Slavophiles and the Westerners.

This life, this struggle, received the distant blessings of men so far apart as Khomjakov and Kireevskij, on the one hand, and on the other the eloquently Western Herzen, whose stormy political thought will always sound like a Beethoven sonata.

These men did not traffic in the sense of life, but they had spirituality, and in their spare partisan polemics there was more life and more music than in all the writings of Leonid Andreev.

· XIII ·

Komissarzhevskaja[38]

My desire is to speak not about myself but to track down the age, the noise and the germination of time. My memory is inimical to all that is personal. If it depended on me, I should only make a wry face in remembering the past. I was never able to understand the Tolstoys and Aksakovs, all those grandson Bagrovs, enamoured of family archives with their epic domestic memoirs. I repeat—my memory is not loving but inimical, and it labors not to reproduce but to distance the past. A *raznochinets*[39] needs no memory—it is enough for him to tell of the books he has read, and his biography is done. Where for happy generations the epic speaks in hexameters and chronicles I have merely the sign of the hiatus, and between me and the age there lies a pit, a moat, filled with clamorous time, the place where a family and reminiscences of a family ought to have been. What was it my family wished to say? I do not know. It was tongue-tied from birth—but it had, nevertheless, something that it might have said. Over my head and over the head of many of my contemporaries there hangs congenital tongue-tie. We were not taught to speak but to babble—and only by listening to the swelling noise of the age and the bleached foam on the crest of its wave did we acquire a language.

A revolution is itself life and death and cannot endure idle chatter about life and death in its presence. Its throat is parched with thirst, but it would not accept a single drop of moisture from alien hands. Nature—revolution—eternal thirst—inflammation (perhaps it envies those ages when thirst was quenched in a quiet home-like way by simply going off to the place where the sheep were watered. This apprehensiveness is characteristic of revolution, this dread of receiving anything at all from the hands of others; it dares not, it is afraid to approach the sources of existence.).

But what did these "sources of existence" ever do for the revolution? Very indifferent was the flow of their rounded waves! For themselves they flowed, for themselves they joined together to form a current, for themselves they boiled and spouted! ("For me, for me, for me," says the revolution. "On your own, on your own, on your own," answers the world.)

Komissarzhevskaja had the straight back of a girl student, a small head, and a little voice that was made for church singing. Bravich played Judge Brack and Komissarzhevskaja was Hedda. She found walking and sitting tedious. The result was that she always stood. She would, for instance, walk up to the blue lantern in the window of Ibsen's professorial parlor and stand there for a long, long time, her flat, slightly stooped back turned to the audience. What was the secret of Komissarzhevskaja's charm? Why

was she such a leader, a kind of Joan of Arc? Why, alongside her, did Savina seem to be an expiring *grande dame*,
exhausted by a shopping trip?

The truth of the matter is that Komissarzhevskaja expressed the Protestant spirit of the Russian intelligentsia,
the peculiar Protestantism of its views on art and the
theater. Not for nothing was she drawn to Ibsen and raised
to heights of virtuosity in that professorial drama with its
Protestant decorum. The intelligentsia never loved the
theater and strove to celebrate its cult in the most modest
and decorous way possible. Komissarzhevskaja went to
meet this Protestantism in the theater halfway, but she
went too far and, exceeding the bounds of the Russian,
became almost European. To begin with, she discarded all
theatrical trumpery: the heat of candles, the red flowerbeds
of the orchestra seats, the satin nests of the loges. A wooden
amphitheater, white walls, gray hangings—clean as a yacht
and bare as a Lutheran church. Komissarzhevskaja had,
nevertheless, all the gifts of a great tragic actress, but they
were in embryonic form. Unlike the Russian actors of that
day—and also, perhaps, of the present day—Komissarzhevskaja possessed an inner sense of music; she raised and
lowered her voice just as the breathing of the verbal se-
quence required. Her acting was three-quarters verbal and
was accompanied only by the most essential, spare gestures,
and even of these there were not many—things like wring-
ing the hands above the head. In creating the plays of
Ibsen and Maeterlinck, she was groping for the European
drama, and she was sincerely convinced that Europe could
offer nothing better and greater than that.

The rosy meat pies of the Aleksandrinskij Theater seemed
so out of harmony with that incorporeal, spectral little
world where it was always Lent. Komissarzhevskaja's small
theater itself was exclusively surrounded by an atmosphere
of sectarian devotion. I do not think that any perspectives
for the future of the theater were opened up here. That

chamber drama came to us from little Norway. Photographers. *Privatdocents*. Civil servants. The comical tragedy of a lost manuscript. The apothecary from Christiania was able to lure a storm into a professor's hen-house and to raise to the heights of tragedy the ominously polite squabbling of Hedda and Brack. For Komissarzhevskaja Ibsen was a foreign hotel, nothing more. Komissarzhevskaja broke out of the ordinary run of Russian theatrical life as out of a madhouse. She was free, but the heart of the theater was coming-to a stop.

When Blok was leaning down over the deathbed of the Russian theater he recalled the name Carmen—that is to say, that from which Komissarzhevskaja could not have been more distant. The days and hours of her small theater were always numbered. Here they breathed the false and impossible oxygen of a theatrical miracle. Blok laughed maliciously at this theatrical miracle in his *Puppet Show*, and when Komissarzhevskaja produced *The Puppet Show* she mocked herself. Amid the grunting and roaring, the whining and declamation, her voice, kin to the voice of Blok, grew stronger and more mature. The theater has lived and will live by the human voice. Petrushka presses to the roof of his mouth a leaf of copper in order to alter his voice. Better Petrushka than Carmen and Aïda, than the pig snout of declamation.

· XIV ·

In a Fur Coat Above One's Station

Towards midnight the waves of a snowstorm were raging along the streets of the Vasilij Island. Blue house lamps in their mica boxes glowed at the corners and crossroads. The bakery shops, unconstrained by regular hours of trade, exhaled a rich steam onto the street, but the watch-makers had long ago closed their shops, filled with a fever-ish muttering and the murmur of cicadas.

Clumsy doormen, bears with badges, dozed at their gates.

That is how it was a quarter of a century ago. Even now, the raspberry globes of pharmacies burn there in the winter.

My companion, emerging from his literary lair of an apartment, from his crypt-apartment with its green myopic lamp and its trough of an ottoman, with its study where the miserly hoard of books threatened to avalanche like the crumbling walls of a ravine, emerging from an apartment where the tobacco seemed to smell of wounded pride—my companion became downright cheerful and, wrapping himself in a fur coat that was above his station in life, turned upon me his ruddy, prickly, Russo-Mongolian face.

He did not summon a cabby. He bellowed for a cabby with such an imperious and chilling stentorian blast that one would have thought such a cry intended for an entire kennel of huskies plus several troikas, not the quilted little nag of a cabby.

Night. The *raznochinets littérateur* in the fur coat above his station in life is angry. Oho! But that is an old acquaint-ance of mine! Under the film of waxed paper in the works of Leont'ev there is a portrait of some spiny beast in a tall fur cap like a mitre—the high priest of frost and the state. Theory scrapes on the frost like the runners of the cabby's sleigh. Are you cold, Byzantium? Shivering and raging is the *raznochinets* author in the fur coat above his station in life.

That was just the way the Novgorodians and Pskovians used to be depicted as raging on their ikons; in tiers on each other's heads stood the laity, to the right and left, disputing and scolding, in astonishment turning their wise peasant heads on short necks toward the event. The beefy faces and hard beards of the disputants were turned toward the event with malign amazement. I think I can discern in them the archetype of literary spite.

As the Novgorodians voted spitefully with their beards on the ikon of the Last Judgment, so literature rages for a century and glowers at the event with the ardent slant-eyed gaze of a *raznochinets* and chronic failure, with the spite of a lay brother who had been awakened too late, summoned, or better to say dragged by the hair to be a witness in the Byzantine court of history.

Literary spite! Were it not for you, what should I have to eat the salt of the earth with?

You are the seasoning for the unleavened bread of understanding, you are the joyful consciousness of injustice, you are the conspiratorial salt which is transmitted with a malicious bow from decade to decade, in a cut-glass salt cellar, with a serving cloth! That is why I so love to extinguish the heat of literature with frost and the barbed stars. Will it crunch like the crust of snow? Will it brighten up in the frosty weather of the Nekrasovian street? If it is genuine, the answer is yes.

To remember not living people but the plaster casts struck from their voices. To go blind. To feel and recognize by hearing. Sad fate! Thus does one penetrate into the present, into the modern age, as via the bed of a dried-up river.

And, you know, those were not friends, not near ones, but alien, distant people! Still, it is only with the masks of other men's voices that the bare walls of my house are decorated. To remember—to make one's way alone back up the dried riverbed!

The first literary encounter is irremediable. That was a man with a parched throat. The nightingales of Fet have long ago boiled away: an alien, patrician pastime. A subject of envy. Lyric. "Mounted or afoot" . . . "The grand piano was fully open." . . . "And by the burning salt of imperishable words."

The painful, inflamed eyelids of Fet drove away sleep. Tjutchev entered the veins like an early sclerosis, like a layer of lime. The five or six last Symbolist words, like the five fish of the gospel, were dragging away the basket, and among them was the big fish: Existence.

But one could not feed the hungry time with them and it was necessary to throw all five out of the basket, including the large dead fish Existence.

At the end of an historic era abstract concepts always stink like rotten fish. Better the wicked and gay sibilance of Russian verse.

The person who had bellowed for a cabby was V.V. Gippius,[40] a teacher of literature, who taught children not literature but the far more interesting science of literary spite. Why did he puff himself up in front of the children? Surely children have no need of the sting of pride, the reptilian hiss of the literary anecdote?

Even then I knew that there gather around literature its witnesses, the members, so to speak, of its household—take, just for example, the Pushkinists and so on. Later I got to know some of them. How vapid they were in comparison with V.V.!

He differed from the other witnesses of literature precisely in this malign astonishment. He had a kind of feral relationship to literature, as if it were the only source of animal warmth. He warmed himself against literature, he rubbed against it with his fur, the ruddy bristle of his hair and his unshaven cheeks. He was a Romulus who hated his wolf mother and, hating her, taught others to love her.

To arrive at V.V.'s place almost inevitably meant to wake him up. Crushing an old copy of *The Scales* or *Northern Flowers* or *The Scorpion*, he would sleep on the hard divan in his study, poisoned by Sologub, wounded by Brjusov, recalling in his sleep Sluchevskij's savage poetry, his poem "Execution in Geneva," the comrade of Konevskoj and

Dobroljubov,[41] those belligerent young monks of early Symbolism.

The hibernation of V.V. was a literary protest, something like a continuation of the policy of the old *Scales* and *Scorpion*. Awakened, he would puff himself up and begin asking about this and that with a malign little smile. But his real conversation consisted of a simple picking over of literary names and books with a kind of animal greed, with a mad but noble envy.

He was inclined to worry about his health and of all diseases he most feared tonsillitis, which prevents one from talking.

It was, nevertheless, in the energy and articulation of his speech that one found all the strength of his personality. He was unconsciously attracted to the sibilant and hissing sounds and to "t" in word endings. To put it in learned terms: a predilection for the dentals and palatals.

Inspired by the happy example of V.V. I still conceive of early Symbolism as a dense thicket of these *shch* sounds. "Nado mnoj orly, orly govorjashchie" (Above my head eagles, eagles speaking). Thus my teacher gave his preference to the patriarchal and warlike consonants of pain and attack, insult and self-defense. For the first time I felt the joy of the outward disharmony of Russian speech when V.V. took it into his head to read to us children the *Firebird* of Fet. "Na suku izvilistom i chudnom" (On the sinuous, miraculous branch): it was as if snakes were hanging above the school desks, a whole forest of sibilant snakes.* The hibernation of V.V. frightened and attracted me.

* It would be appropriate here to recall another of the intimates of literature's house and a declaimer of poetry whose personality was reflected with extraordinary force in the peculiarities of the pronunciation—N. V. Nedobrovo.

A mordantly polite Petersburger, loquacious frequenter of the salons of late Symbolism, impenetrable as a young clerk

But surely literature is not a bear sucking its paws, not a heavy sleep on the study sofa after work?

I would come to him to wake up the beast of literature. To listen to him growl, to watch him toss and turn. I would come to my teacher of "Russian" at home. The whole savor of the thing lay in that coming to him "at home." Even now it is difficult for me to free myself from the notion that I was then at literature's own house. Never again was literature to be a house, an apartment, a family where red-haired little boys slept side by side in their netted cribs.

Beginning as early as Radishchev and Novikov, V.V. had established personal relations with Russian writers, splenetic and loving liaisons filled with noble enviousness, jealousy, with jocular disrespect, grievous unfairness—as is customary between the members of one family.

An intellectual builds the temple of literature with immovable idols. Korolenko, for example, who wrote so much about the Komi, seems to me to have turned himself into a little tin god of the Komi. V.V. taught that one should build literature not as a temple but as a gens. What he prized in literature was the patriarchal, paternal principle of culture.

How good it is that I managed to love not the priestly flame of the ikon lamp but the ruddy little flame of literary (V.V.G.) spite!

The judgments of V.V. continue to hold me in their power down to the present day. The grand tour which I

---

guarding a state secret, Nedobrovo turned up everywhere to recite Tjutchev—almost, as it were, to intercede for him. His speech, which was, anyway, most extraordinarily clear, with wide open vowels, as if it were inscribed on silver phonograph records, became astonishingly brilliant when he read Tjutchev, especially the alpine lines of "A kotoryj god beleet" and "A zarja i nynche seet." Then began a veritable flood of open a's— it seemed as though the speaker had just washed his throat with a draught of cold alpine water.

made with him through the patriarchate of Russian literature from the Novikov-Radishchev period all the way to
the Konevits[42] of early Symbolism, has remained the only
one. After that, I merely "read a bit."

In place of a necktie there dangled a piece of string. His
short neck, subject to tonsillitis, moved nervously in the
colored, unstarched collar. From his larynx were torn sibilant, gurgling sounds: the belligerent *shch* and *t*.

It seemed as though this person was forever suffering
the final agony, belligerent and passionate. Something of
the death agony was in his very nature, and this tortured
and agitated him, nourishing the drying roots of his spiritual being.

By the way, something like the following conversation
was a commonplace in the Symbolist milieu:

"How do you do, Ivan Ivanovich?"

"Oh, all right, Pëtr Petrovich. I live in the hour of my
death."

V.V. loved poems in which there were such energetic
and happy rhymes as *plamen'* (flame)—*kamen'* (stone),
ljubov' (love)—*krov'* (blood), *plot'* (flesh)—*Gospod'*
(Lord).

His vocabulary was, without his being conscious of it,
controlled by two words: *bytie* (existence) and *plamen'*
(flame). If the entire Russian language were given over to
his keeping, I seriously think that he would, out of care-
lessness, burn it up, destroy the whole Russian lexicon to
the glory of *bytie* and *plamen'*.

The literature of the century was well born. Its house
was a full cup.[43] At the broad open table the guests sat
with Walsingham.[44] New guests, throwing off their fur
coats, came in out of the cold. The little blue flames on the
punch reminded the new arrivals of pride, friendship, and
death. Around the table flew the request which, it seemed,
was always being uttered for the last time—"Sing, Mary"—
the anguished request of the last banquet.

But not less dear to me than the beautiful girl who sang that shrill Scottish song was the one who, in a hoarse voice worn out with talk, asked her for the song.

If I had a vision of Konstantin Leont'ev yelling for a cabby on that snow-covered street of the Vasilij Island it was only because he of all Russian writers is most given to handling time in lumps. He feels centuries as he feels the weather, and he shouts at them.

He might have shouted, "Oh, fine, what a splendid century we have!"—something like "A nice dry day it turned out!" Only it didn't turn out that way! He was struck dumb. The hard frost burned his throat, and the peremptory shout at the century froze like a column of mercury.

Looking back at the entire nineteenth century of Russian culture—shattered, finished, unrepeatable, which no one must repeat, which no one dares repeat—I wish to hail the century, as one would hail settled weather, and I see in it the unity lent it by the measureless cold which welded decades together into one day, one night, one profound winter, within which the terrible State glowed, like a stove, with ice.

And in this wintry period of Russian history, literature, taken at large, strikes me as something patrician, which puts me out of countenance: with trembling I lift the film of waxed paper above the winter cap of the writer. No one is to blame in this and there is nothing to be ashamed of. A beast must not be ashamed of its furry hide. Night furred him. Winter clothed him. Literature is a beast. The furriers—night and winter.

Theodosia

·1925·

· I ·

The Harbor Master

THE starched white tunic inherited from the old regime made him look miraculously younger and reconciled him with himself: the freshness of a gymnasium student and the brisk cheerfulness of an executive—a combination of qualities which he prized in himself and feared to lose. He conceived of the entire Crimea as one blinding, stiffly starched geographical tunic. On the other side of Perekop was night. There beyond the salt marshes there was no longer any starch, there were no washerwomen, no glad subordination, and it would be impossible there to have that springy step, as after a swim, that permanent excitement: the blended sense of well-bought currency, of clear government service and, at the age of forty, the feeling of having passed one's exams.

Conditions were only too favorable. The businesslike briefcase was arranged with the easy domestic elegance of a travelling case, with little recesses for razor, soap dish, and brushes of various kinds. Without him, that is without the harbor master, there passed not one single ton for the barley men and the wheat men, not one ton for the grain shippers, not even for Rosh himself, the commissioner of yesterday, today an upstart, nor for the legendary Kanitfershtan, lazy and languid in the Italian manner, who shipped barley to Marseilles, nor for the wheaty Lifschitz, a scrawny turkey, the minister of the public garden of Ajvazovskij, nor to the Tsentrosojuz,[45] nor to the Reisners, whose affairs were going so well that instead of their silver they celebrated their golden wedding anniversary, and the father, out of happiness, fraternized with the son.

Each of the filthy steamers, smelling of the kitchen and

soya, with a crew of mulattoes, and with a captain's cabin that was thoroughly heated, like the international sleeper, but more like the garret of a well-to-do doorman, carried away his tons, too, indistinguishably mixed with the others.

People knew perfectly well that they were selling, along with the grain, the land on which they walked, but they went on selling that land, observing how it crumbled into the sea, and counting on leaving when they should feel under their feet the last slip of the sinking earth.

Whenever the harbor master walked along the densely shaded Italian Street, beloved by its old residents, he was stopped every minute, taken by the arm, and led aside—which was, by the way, one of the customs of the city, where all matters were decided on the street and no one knew on leaving home when he would reach or even whether he would reach the place he had set out for. And he had developed the habit of talking with everyone just about as he would have talked with the wife of a superior —inclining his ovoid head to one side, keeping always to the left—so that the person to whom he was talking was from the outset grateful and embarrassed.

He would greet certain of the elect as if they were old friends returning from a long voyage, and would award them juicy kisses. He carried these kisses about with him like a box of fresh peppermints.

At nightfall, since I did not belong to the respected citizenry of Theodosia, I would knock at various doors in search of a place to bed down. The northeast wind was raging in the toy streets. The Ginsbergs, the Landsbergs, et al. drank their tea with white Jewish *chale* bread. The Tartar nightwatchmen walked about under the windows of money-changing shops and secondhand stores, where chibouks and guitars were draped in the silk dressing-gown of a colonel. Occasionally, too, there would pass by a belated company of cadets thundering with the soles of their English boots and rending the air with a certain paean containing several indecent expressions, which were omitted during the day at the insistence of the local rabbi.

It was then that I would rush about, in the fever familiar to every wanderer, searching for a place to sleep. And Aleksandr Aleksandrovich would open to me as a nightly asylum the harbor administration office.

I think there never was a stranger lodging. At the sound of the electric bell the door was opened by a drowsy, secretly hostile servant, made of canvas. The bright light bulbs, white as sugar, flashed on, lighting up vast maps of the Crimea, tables of ocean depths and currents, diagrams and chronometric clocks. I would carefully remove the bronze inkstand from the conference table, covered with a green cloth. Here it was warm and clean, as in a surgical ward. All the English and Italian ships that had ever awakened Aleksandr Aleksandrovich were registered in journals and lay sleeping like bibles on the shelves.

In order to understand what Theodosia was like under Denikin and Wrangel, one must know what it was like before. It was the particular quirk of this city to pretend that nothing had changed, that everything remained just exactly as it had always been. And in old times the city resembled not Genoa, that nest of military and mercantile predators, but gentle Florence. In the observatory at Harbor Master Sarandinaki's, the recording of the weather and plotting of isotherms were not the only activities: there were also weekly gatherings to hear plays and poetry, both by Sarandinaki himself and by other inhabitants of the city. The Chief of Police himself once wrote a play. Mabo,[46] the director of the Azov Bank, was better known as a poet. And when Voloshin used to appear in the pock-marked roadways of Theodosia in his town outfit—woolen stockings, velveteen trousers, and velvet jacket—the city was seized by a sort of classical melting mood, and merchants ran out of their shops.

There's no disputing it: we should be grateful to Wrangel

for letting us breathe the pure air of a lawless sixteenth-century Mediterranean republic. But it was not easy for Attic Theodosia to adjust herself to the severe rule of the Crimean pirates.

That is why she cherished her kindly patron, Aleksandr Aleksandrovich, that sea-kitten in a tropical cork helmet, a man who, blinking sweetly, looked history in the face and answered its insolent tricks with a gentle meow. He was, however, the sea-god of the city—in his own way, Neptune. The more powerful the man, the more significant his manner of getting up. The French kings did not even get up, but *rose*, like the sun, and that not once but twice: the "small" and "great" rising. Aleksandr Aleksandrovich awoke together with the sea. But how did he keep in touch with the sea? He kept in touch with the sea by telephone. In the half light of his office there was a gleam of English razors and the smell of fresh linen and strong eau de Cologne and of a sweetish imported tobacco. These splendid masculine sleeping quarters, which would have been the envy of any American, were nevertheless a captain's deck-house and the hub of maritime communications.

Aleksandr Aleksandrovich would awake with the first steamer. Two aides, orderlies in white sailcloth, as schooled in their work as hospital attendants, would burst into head-long action at the first telephone bell and whisper to the chief, who at that moment resembled a drowsy kitten, that there had arrived and was anchored in the roads some English, Turkish, or even Serbian steamer. Aleksandr Aleksandrovich opened tiny little eyes and, though he was powerless to change anything about the arrival of the ship, said, "Ah! Good! Very good!" Then the ship became a citizen of the roads, the civic day of the sea got under way, and the harbor master changed from a sleeping kitten into the protector of merchants, into the inspirer of the customs house and of the fountain of the stock exchange, into the cognac god, the thread god, the currency god—in short, into the civic god of the sea. There was in him something of the swallow, fretting with housewifely concern over her nest—for the time being. And you would not notice that she was training with her little ones for a flight over the Atlantic. For him evacuation was not a catastrophe nor a chance occurrence, but a joyous flight across the Atlantic (according to his instinct as a father and family man); it was, so to speak, the triumph of his lifelong resiliency. He never said anything about it, but he prepared for it, perhaps unconsciously, from the first moment.

· II ·

The Old Woman's Bird

At the farther end of Italian Street, beyond the last secondhand store, past the abandoned gallery of the Gostin-nyj Dvor, where there was formerly a carpet auction, behind the little French house, ivy covered and with jalousies, where the theosophist Anna Mikhajlovna starved to death in the upholstered parlor, the road takes an upward turn toward the quarantine quarter.

From January on, the winter became extraordinarily harsh. Heavy artillery was transported along the ice at frozen Perekop. In the coffeehouse next door to the Astoria, English soldiers—"bobbies"[47]—set up a warming station. They sat in a circle around the brazier, warmed their large red hands, sang Scottish songs, and so crowded the delicate proprietors that they were prevented from cooking coffee and frying eggs. Warm and gentle, the sheep-spirited city was turned into hell. The honorary village idiot, a merry, black-beared Karaite, no longer ran about the streets with his retinue of urchins.

The quarantine quarter: a labyrinth of little low-lying clay walled houses with tiny windows, zigzag lanes with clay fences as tall as a man, where one stumbled over ice-covered rope or into cornel bushes. A pitiful clay Herculaneum just dug out of the earth and guarded by ill-tempered dogs. During the day you walked through this little city as though following the plan of dead Rome, and at night, in the impenetrable gloom, you were ready to knock at the door of any *petite bourgeoise* if only she would shelter you from the vicious dogs and let you in where the samovar was. The life of the quarantine district was centered about the concern for water. It guarded as the apple of its eye its ice-covered pumphouse. The noise of a clamorous female assembly never subsided on the steep hillock where the jets of pumped water had no time to freeze, and where, to keep the buckets from overflowing when they were raised, filled to the brim, the old women sealed their icy burden with floats of fagots.

The idyl of quarantine lasted several days. In one of the clay huts I rented a room from an old woman for the price of a hen's egg. Like all the housewives of the quarantine quarter, the old woman lived in the festive cleanliness of one about to die. She did not simply tidy her little house, she purified it. In the hallway there was a tiny washbowl, but so miserly was the flow of water that there was not the faintest possibility of milking it to the end. There was the smell of bread, of the burnt kerosene in a dull nursery lamp, and of the pure breath of old people. The clock ticked ponderously. Like large grains of salt, the winter stars were sprinkled about the court. And I was glad that the room was warm with breath, that someone was pottering about behind the wall, preparing a meal of potatoes, onions, and a handful of rice. The old woman kept her tenant like a bird: she thought it necessary to change his water, clean out his cage, and scatter some grain. At that time it was better to be a bird than a man, and the temptation to become the old woman's bird was enormous.

When Denikin was retreating from Kursk, the military authorities herded the railroad workers and their families together, put them into heated cars, and before they realized what was going on they were rolling off to the Black Sea. Now these railroad birds[48] from Kursk, taken from their comfortable roost, had settled in the quarantine, made themselves at home, cleaned their pots with bricks, but had still not recovered from their astonishment. The old woman could not talk without a superstitious horror of how they had been "taken down from Kursk," but as for talk about being taken back, there was none, since it was irreversibly supposed that they had been brought here to die.

If one went outside on one of those icy Crimean nights and listened to the noise of footsteps on the snowless clayey earth, frozen solid like our northern wheel tracks in October, if in the darkness one groped with the eyes among the city's hills—populated sepulchres, but with extinguished lights—if one swallowed that gruel of smothered life, thickened with dense barking of dogs and salted with stars, one began to sense with physical clarity the plague that had descended upon the world, a Thirty Years' War, with pestilence, darkened lamps, barking of dogs, and, in the houses of little people, appalling silence.

· III ·

The Royal Mantle of the Law[49]

Breath, condensed in droplets, settled on the yellow walls of the bathhouse. Tiny black cups, guarded by sweating glasses of ferriferous Crimean water, were arranged as bait for the red snout-like lips of Karaites and Greeks. There where two were sitting a third immediately planted himself, and behind the third, suspiciously and as if for no reason at all, there stood two more. The little groups scattered and resolved like tumors, governed by the peculiar law of the gravitation of flies: people clung round the unseen center, buzzing and hanging above a piece of invisible sugar, and dashed away with malicious whining from some deal that had fallen through.

The dirty little newspaper of the OSVAG,[50] printed on gray pulp that always looked like proof sheets, called up impressions of Russian autumn in the shop of a petty merchant.

Meanwhile, above the fly-weddings and braziers, the life of the city proceeded along large, clean lines. From the Mithradates—the ancient Persian fortress on a stone mountain resembling cardboard stage-setting—to the long arrow of the breakwater and the strictly genuine backdrop of highway, prison, and bazaar, the city described the aerial flanks of a triangle formation of cranes and offered to negotiate peace between the earth, sky, and sea. As in most of the amphitheatrical cities of the southern coast, its light blue and gray flocks of gleefully stupid houses ran down from the mountain like a consignment of sheep.

The city was older, better, and cleaner than anything that was going on in it. No dirt stuck to it. Into its splendid body bit the pincers of prison and barracks, along its street walked cyclopes in black felt boots, *sotniks*,[51] smelling of dog and wolf, guardsmen of the defeated army, wearing service caps and infected to the soles of their shoes with the foxy electricity of health and youth. On some people the possibility of committing murder with impunity acts like a fresh mineral bath, and for such people, with their childishly impudent and dangerously empty brown eyes, the Crimea was simply a spa where they were following a course of treatment, keeping to a stimulating and salutary regime, suited to the requirements of their nature.

Colonel Tsygal'skij played nursemaid to his sister, feeble-minded and lachrymose, and to the eagle—the sick, pitiful, blind, broken-clawed eagle of the Volunteer Army. In one corner of his quarters the emblematic eagle, as it were, pottered about invisibly to the tune of the hissing primus stove, and in the other, wrapped in an overcoat or a down shawl, huddled his sister, looking like a mad clairvoyant. His extra pair of patent leather boots cried out to go—not, like seven-league boots, to Moscow—but to be sold at the bazaar. Tsygal'skij was born to nurse someone and especially to guard someone's sleep. Both he and his sister looked like blind people, but in the colonel's eyes, bright with agate blackness and feminine kindness, there stagnated the dark resolve of a leader, while his sister's contained only bovine terror. He gave his sister grapes and rice to eat and would sometimes bring home from the cadet academy certain modest ration packets, which reminded one of the food rations given out to intellectuals and those who lived in the House of Scholars.

It is difficult to imagine why such people are necessary in any army at all. Such a man would be capable, I think, of throwing his arms around a general at some critical moment and saying, "Forget it, my dear fellow—let's rather go to my place and have a talk." Tsygal'skij used to go to the cadets to lecture on gunnery like a student going to his lesson.

Once—embarrassed by his voice, the primus stove, his sister, the unsold patent leather boots and the bad tobacco—he read some verses aloud. There was the awkward expression, "I care not: without the throne or with the czar . . ." and some further wishes about the kind of Russia he needed—"crowned with the royal mantle of the Law"—and so on, all reminding one of the rain-blackened Themis on the Senate in Petersburg.

"Whose poem is that?"

"Mine."

Then he revealed to me that somnambulistic landscape in which he lived. The chief feature of this landscape was the abyss that had opened up where Russia had been. The Black Sea extended all the way to the Neva: its waves, thick as pitch, licked at the slabs of the Isaac Cathedral and broke with mournful foam against the steps of the Senate. In this wild expanse, somewhere between Kursk and Sevastopol, swam the royal mantle of the Law, as if it were a lifebuoy, and it was not volunteers but some sort of fishermen in canoes who salvaged this queer appurtenance of the governmental toilet, about which the colonel himself could scarcely have known or guessed before the revolution.

The colonel: a nursemaid decked in the royal mantle of the Law!

....

· IV ·

Mazesa da Vinci

....

When a phaeton with empty seats like plush medallions or a one-horse break with a wedding-pink canopy made its way into the scorching backwater of the upper town, the clopping hooves could be heard four blocks away. The horse, sweeping sparks with its legs, belabored the hot stones with such force that it seemed as if a staircase must be formed of them.

It was so dry there that a lizard would have died of thirst. A man in sandals and green socks, overcome by the appearance of the thundering carriage, stood looking after it for a long time. His face showed such astonishment one would have thought they were carting uphill the hitherto unused lever of Archimedes. Then he walked up to a woman who was sitting in her apartment and bartering goods right out of the window, which she had turned into a counter. After tapping a melon with his silver gypsy ring, he asked that it be cut in half for him. But when he had gone as far as the corner, he came back, exchanged the melon for two homemade cigarettes, and quickly made off.

In the upper town the houses have to a certain extent the character of barracks or bastions; they give the pleasant impression of stability and also of natural age, equal to that of human life. Leaving aside archeology and not very remote antiquity, they were the first to turn this rough land into a city.

The house of the parents of Mazesa da Vinci, the artist, shamefully turned its domestic and lively rear toward the stone quarry. Soiled biblical featherbeds sprawled in the hot sun. Rabbits melted like sterilized down, running this way and that, spreading over the ground like spilled milk. And not too far, not too near, but right where it had to be, stood the hospitable booth with its door flung wide open. On the slanting yardarms of twine there flapped an enormous wash. The virtuous armada progressed under martial, maternal sail, but the wing belonging to Mazesa was overwhelming in the brilliance and wealth of its rigging: black and raspberry blouses, silk ankle-length night shirts, such as are worn by newlyweds and angels, one of zephyr cloth, one à la Beethoven—I am of course speaking only of the shirts—and one resembling evening dress with long ape-like arms to which had been added some homemade cuffs.

Laundry dries quickly in the south: Mazesa walked straight into the yard, and ordered all that to be taken down and ironed at once.

He chose his name himself, and to those who inquired

about it he would reply only reluctantly with the explanation that he liked the name da Vinci. In the first half of his sobriquet—Mazesa—he retained a blood link with his family: his father, a small, very decent man, having no fear of seasickness, transported drapery goods to Kerch in a powered sailboat, and he was called simply Mr. Mazes. And thus Mazesa, with the addition of the feminine ending, turned the family name into his first name.

Who does not know of the shipboard chaos of the renowned Leonardo's studio? Objects swirled in a whirlwind in the three dimensions of his ingenious workshop; pigeons got in through the dormer window and soiled with their droppings precious brocade, and in his prophetic blindness the master stumbled against the humble articles of everyday life of the Renaissance. Mazesa inherited from his involuntary godfather this fruitful uproar of the three dimensions, and his bedroom resembled a Renaissance vessel under sail.

From the ceiling there hung a large cradle basket in which Mazesa liked to rest during the day. Light flocks of down luxuriated in the dense, noble blackness. A ladder, brought into the room by the stubborn whim of Mazesa, was placed against the entresol, where there stood out among an assorted inventory the framework of some heavy bronze lamps that had hung in the days of Mazesa's grandfather in a Karaite prayer house. From the crater of a porcelain inkstand with sad synagogical lions there protruded several bearded, splintered pens, which had long been unacquainted with ink. On the shelf, under a velvet drape, was his library: a Spanish bible, Makarov's dictionary, Leskov's *Cathedral Folk*, the entomology of Fabre and Baedeker's guide to Paris. On the night table, next to the envelope of an old letter from Argentina, there was a microscope, which gave the false impression that Mazesa would peer into it on waking up in the morning.

In the little city seized by Wrangel's condottieri, Mazesa

was completely unnoticed and happy. He took walks, ate fruit, and swam in the free pool, dreamed of buying the white rubber-soled shoes which had been received at the Tsentrosojuz. His relationship with people and the entire world was built on vagueness and sweet reticence.

He would go down the hill, select in the city some victim, cling to him for two, three, sometimes six hours and, sooner or later, bring him through the scorching zigzag streets back home. In doing this he was, like a tarantula, performing some dark instinctive act peculiar to him alone. He said the same thing to everyone: "Let's go to my place— we have a stone house!" But in the stone house it was the same as in the others: featherbeds, carnelian stones, photographs, and woven napkins.

Mazesa drew only self portraits, and specialized in studies of the Adam's apple.

When the things had been ironed, Mazesa began to get ready for his evening's outing. He didn't wash but passionately immersed himself in the silver girlish mirror. His eyes darkened. His round feminine shoulders trembled.

The white tennis pants, Beethoven shirt, and sport belt did not satisfy him. He took out of the wardrobe his morning coat and in full evening ensemble—unimpeachable from sandals to embroidered skull cap—with black cheviot fins on his white thighs, he went out into the street, already washed in the goat milk of the Theodosia moon.

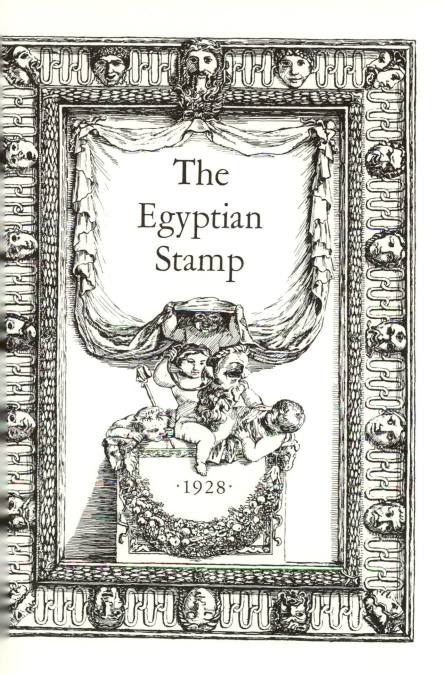

The Egyptian Stamp

·1928·

I do not like rolled-up manuscripts. Some of them are heavy and smeared with time, like the trumpet of the archangel.

· I ·

THE Polish serving girl had gone into the church of Guarenghi[52] to gossip and to pray to the Holy Virgin. That night there had been a dream of a Chinaman, bedecked in ladies' handbags, like a necklace of partridges, and of an American duel in which the opponents fired their pistols at cabinets of chinaware, at inkpots, and at family portraits.

I propose to you, my family, a coat of arms: a glass of boiled water. In the rubbery aftertaste of Petersburg's boiled water I drink my unsuccessful domestic immortality. The centrifugal force of time has scattered our Viennese chairs and Dutch plates with little blue flowers. Nothing is left. Thirty years have passed like a slow fire. For thirty years a cold white flame has licked at the backs of mirrors, where the bailiff's tags are attached.

But how can I tear myself away from you, dear Egypt of objects? The clear eternity of dining room, bedroom, study. With what excuse cover my guilt? You wish Walhalla? The warehouses of Kokorev! Go there for salvation! Already the porters, dancing in horror, are lifting the grand piano (a Mignon) like a lacquered black meteor fallen from the sky. Bast mats are spread like the chasubles of priests. The cheval-glass floats sideways down the staircase, maneuvering its palm-tree length about the landings.

That evening Parnok had hung his morning coat on the back of a Viennese chair so that during the night it might rest its shoulders and arm holes and have out its

sleep in the solid slumber of a cheviot. Who knows? Perhaps on its Viennese chair the morning coat turns somer-
saults, becomes young again—in short, frolics about? This
invertebrate companion of young men pines for the triptych
of mirrors at the fashionable tailor's. At the fitting it had
been a simple sack—something like a knight's armor or a
dubious camisole—which the artistic tailor had covered
with designs in his Pythagorean chalk and inspired with
life and fluent ease:

—Go, my beauty, and live! Strut at concerts, give talks,
love, and make your mistakes!

—Oh, Mervis, Mervis, what have you done? Why have
you deprived Parnok of his earthly shell, why parted him
from his beloved sister?

—Is he asleep?

—He's asleep! The scamp—it's a pity to waste electric
light on him!

The last coffee beans disappeared down the crater of the
coffee-grinder, shaped like a barrel-organ.

The abduction was accomplished.

Mervis carried her off like a Sabine woman.

We count by years, but in reality, in any apartment on
Kamenoostrovskij, time is cleft into dynasties and centuries.

The management of a house is always rather grand. One
cannot embrace the termini of a life: from the moment
when one has comprehended the gothic German alphabet
all the way to the golden fat of the university's *piroshki*.

The proud and touchy odor of gasoline and the greasy
smell of the dear old kerosene protect the apartment,
vulnerable as it is to attack from the kitchen, where porters
break through with their catapults of firewood. Dusty rags
and brushes warm up its white blood.

In the beginning there had been a workbench here—
and Il'in's map of the hemispheres.

From this Parnok drew solace. He was consoled by the linen paper, which could not be torn. Poking with his pen-holder at oceans and continents, he plotted the itineraries of grandiose voyages, comparing the airy outlines of Aryan Europe with the blunt boot of Africa, with inexpressive Australia. In South America, beginning with Patagonia, he also found a certain keenness.

His respect for Il'in's map had remained in Parnok's blood since those fabulous years when he imagined that the aquamarine and ochre hemispheres, like two enormous balls held in the net of latitudes, had been empowered for their visual mission by the white-hot chancellery in the very bowels of the earth and that, like nutritional pills, they contained within themselves condensed space and distance.

Is it not with the same feeling that a singer of the Italian school, preparing to take off on her tour of a still young America, covers the geographical chart with her voice, measures the ocean with its metallic timbre, and checks the inexperienced pulse of the steamship engines with roulades and tremolos . . .

Upside down on the retina of her eye are those same two Americas, like two green gamebags containing Washington and the Amazon. By her maiden voyage on the salt sea she inaugurates the map as she reads her fortune in dollars and Russian hundred-rouble notes with their wintry crunch.

The fifties deceived her. No *bel canto* could have brightened them up. Everywhere the same low sky like a draped ceiling, the same smoky reading rooms, the same lances of the *Times* and the *Gazettes* plunged into the heart's core of the century. And, finally, Russia . . .

Her little ears will begin to tickle: *kreshchatik, shchastie* and *shchavel'.*[53] And her mouth will be stretched to her ears by the unheard of, the impossible sound Ы.

And then the Cavalier Guards will flock to the church of Guarenghi for the singing of the requiem. The golden vultures will rend to pieces the Roman Catholic songstress.

How high they placed her! Could that really be death? Death would not dare to open its mouth in the presence of the diplomatic corps.

—We shall overwhelm her with plumes, with gendarmes, with Mozart!

At this moment the delirious images of the novels of Balzac and Stendhal flitted through his mind: young men in the act of conquering Paris and flicking at their shoes with handkerchiefs as they stand at the entrances of private residences—and off he went to recapture his morning coat.

The tailor Mervis lived on Monetnaja, right next to the lycée, but it was difficult to say whether he worked for the students; that was rather taken for granted, as it is taken for granted that a fisherman on the Rhine catches trout and not some sort of filth. Everything indicated that the mind of Mervis was occupied by something more important than his job as tailor. It was not for nothing that his relatives came running to him from distant places just as his client backed away in stupefaction and repentance.

—Who will give my children their roll and butter? said Mervis, gesturing with his hand as though he were scooping up some butter, and in the birdy air of the tailor's apartment Parnok had a vision not only of butter molded in the shape of a star and crimped with dewy petals but even of a bunch of radishes. Then Mervis cleverly turned the conversation first to the lawyer Grusenberg, who had ordered a senator's uniform from him in January, and then for some reason to his son Aron, a student at the Conservatory, became confused, began to fluster, and plunged behind a partition.

—Well, thought Parnok, perhaps it had to turn out this

THE EGYPTIAN STAMP 155

way. Perhaps the morning coat is no longer here, perhaps he actually did sell it, as he says, to pay for the cheviot.

Furthermore, if one thinks about it, Mervis has no real feeling for the cutting of a morning coat. With him it always turns out to be a frock coat—something obviously more familiar to him.

Lucien de Rubempré[54] wore rough linen underwear and an awkward suit sewn by the village tailor; he ate chestnuts in the street and was terrified of concierges. Once, on a fortunate day for himself, he was shaving when the future came to life in his lather.

Parnok stood alone, forgotten by the tailor Mervis and his family. His gaze fell on the partition, behind which hummed a woman's contralto like viscous Jewish honey. This partition, pasted over with pictures, resembled a rather bizarre iconostasis.

There, dressed in a fur coat and with a distorted face, was Pushkin, whom some gentry resembling torchbearers were carrying out of a carriage, narrow as a sentry box, and, disregarding the astonished coachman in his archbishop's cap, were about to fling into the doorway. Alongside this the old-fashioned pilot of the nineteenth century, Santos-Dumont,[55] in his double-breasted jacket behung with pendants, having been thrown by the play of elements from the basket of his balloon, was depicted hanging by a rope and peering at a soaring condor. There was next a representation of some Dutchmen on stilts, who were running all about their little country like cranes.

The places where the inhabitants of Petersburg arrange
their rendezvous are not so very different one from the
other. They are hallowed by the remoteness of their origins,
by the sea-green of the sky, and by the Neva. One could
mark them on a map of the city by little crosses amid
the heavy-fleeced parks and cardboard streets. Perhaps they
do change in the course of history, but just before the end,
when the temperature of the age shot up to 37.3 and life
raced out on a false alarm like a fire brigade thundering
through the night along the luminous Nevskij Prospekt,
they could easily be counted:

There was, to begin with, the Empire Pavillion in the
Engineer Garden, where an outsider would have been
ashamed to look in for fear of being involved in affairs
that had nothing to do with him or of being compelled,
for no reason on earth, to sing some Italian aria. Secondly,
there were the Theban sphinxes across from the University. A third was the unsightly arch at the place where
Galernaja Street comes out (not even good as a shelter from
the rain). And, finally, there was a certain side alley in the
Summer Garden, the position of which escapes me, though
every knowledgeable person could immediately point it out
with no difficulty. That is all. Only madmen would insist
on meeting near the Bronze Horseman or the Alexander
Column.

There lived in Petersburg a little man with patent
leather shoes, who was despised by doormen and women.
His name was Parnok. In early spring he would run out
onto the street and patter along the still wet sidewalks
with his little sheep hooves.

His desire was to get a position as a dragoman in the

Ministry of Foreign Affairs, persuade Greece to undertake some risky adventure, and write a memorandum.

In February he fixed the following incident in his mind:

Blocks of good bottom ice were being transported through the city to the creamery. The ice was geometrically whole and salubrious, untouched by death and spring. But on the last sled there floated past a bright green pine branch frozen into the sky-blue glass like a Greek girl in an open grave. The black sugar of the snow lay spread out underfoot, but the trees stood in warm little moons of thawed earth.

A wild parabola joined Parnok with the pompous enfilades of history and music.

—They will throw you out one of these days, Parnok, throw you out with frightful scandal and shame . . . they'll take you by the arm and pf-f-t! . . . out of the Symphony Hall, out of the Society of Friends and Amateurs of the Last Word, out of the Circle for Grasshopper Music, out of the salon of Mme. Bookbinder . . . who knows where else? . . . but out you will go, disgraced, vilified . . .

He had certain false memories: for example, he was convinced that when he was a child he had once stolen into a sumptuous conference hall and turned on the lights. All the clusters of bulbs and bunches of candles with crystal icicles had suddenly flashed out like a vacant apiary. The electricity had gushed out in such a terrifying current that it hurt his eyes, and he burst into tears.

Dear, blind, egotistical light.

He loved woodpiles and cordwood. In winter a dry log ought to be resonant, light, and hollow. And the birch should have a lemon-yellow core and weigh no more than a frozen fish. He felt a log as if it were alive in his hand.

From childhood he had been devoted to whatever was useless, metamorphosing the streetcar rattle of life into events of consequence, and when he began to fall in love he tried to tell women about this, but they did not understand him, for which he revenged himself by speaking to them in a wild, bombastic birdy language and exclusively about the loftiest matters.

Shapiro was called Nikolaj Davydych. Whence this "Nikolaj" had come was not known, but its being linked to the name Davyd struck us as charming. It seemed to me that Davydovich—i.e., Shapiro himself—had drawn his head back into his shoulders and was bowing to some Nikolaj from whom he wanted to borrow money.

Shapiro depended on my father. He would sit for hours in the absurd study with its copying machine and the arm-chair *style russe*. Of Shapiro it was said that he was honest and "a little man." I was for some reason convinced that "little people" never spent more than three roubles and always lived in the Sands.[56] The big-headed Nikolaj Davydovich was a rough and kindly guest, eternally rubbing his hands together and smiling guiltily like an errand boy admitted into the house. He smelled of tailor and iron.

I was confident that Shapiro was honest and, delighted by this knowledge, secretly hoped that no one else would dare to be so. Below Shapiro on the social ladder there were only the commercial messengers—those mysterious runners whom one sent to the bank and to Kaplan. Threads passed from Shapiro through the commercial messengers to the bank and to Kaplan.

I loved Shapiro for needing my father. The Sands, where he lived, was a Sahara surrounding the dressmaking studio of his wife. My head swam at the thought there were people who depended on Shapiro. I feared that a tornado might develop in the Sands and sweep away his seamstress wife with her single employee and the children with their infected throats—all like a little feather, like three roubles.

At night, as I lay falling asleep on my sagging mattress by the blue gleam of the night light, I pondered what to do with Shapiro: should I present him a camel and a carton of dates so that he might not perish in the Sands, or take him, together with that martyr, Mme. Shapiro, to the Kazan cathedral, where the rent air was black and sweet?

There is an obscure heraldry of moral ideas going all the way back to childhood: the ripping sound of a torn cloth can signify honesty, and the cold of madapollam cloth— holiness.

But the barber, holding above Parnok's head a pyramidal flask of Piksafon, poured the cold, brown liquid right onto his crown, which had gone bald at Scriabin's concerts— sloshed his head with that freezing sacramental oil—and Parnok, feeling the icy slap on the top of his skull, came to life. A frosty little shiver, as at a concert, ran along his dry skin and—Mother, have pity on your son!— penetrated beneath his collar.

—Not too hot? asked the barber as he followed the above treatment by dousing his head with a watering can full of boiling water, but Parnok only squinted his eyes and plunged his head deeper into the marble chopping block of the lavatory.

And his rabbit blood was instantly warmed under the shaggy towel.

Parnok was the victim of his preconceptions as to how a love affair must proceed.

On laid paper, my dear sirs, on English laid paper with water marks and deckle edge he informed the unsuspecting lady that the distance between the Millionnaja, the Admiralty, and the Summer Garden had been polished like the carat of a diamond and brought to full combat readiness.

Such paper, dear reader, could have served for the correspondence of the Hermitage caryatids—for their notes of sympathy or esteem.

There are indeed people in the world who have never

been ill with anything more dangerous than influenza
and are somehow hooked on to the present age sideways,
like artificial corsages at a dance. Such people never feel
themselves to be grown up and, at thirty, are still finding
someone to be offended by, someone whose apologies they
require. They were never particularly spoiled by anyone,
and yet they are as corrupt as if they had received the
academic ration of sardines and chocolate all their lives.
They are muddle-headed people who know nothing more
than a few chess moves but are still eager for a game just
to see how it will turn out. They ought to spend their
whole lives somewhere in a villa among agreeable acquaintances, listening to the chink of cups on the balcony,
around the samovar that someone has fired with pine cones,
and chatting with crab venders and letter carriers. I should
like to collect them all and settle them in Sestroretsk
(since there is no longer anywhere else).

Parnok was a man of Kamenoostrovskij Prospekt—one
of the lightest and most irresponsible streets of Petersburg.
In 1917, after the February days, this street became still
lighter with its steam laundries, its Georgian shops, where
even cocoa was still to be bought, and its maniacal automobiles, the property of the Provisional Government.

Venture neither to the right nor to the left: there is
bedlam, there is streetcar-less backwater. But on Kamenoostrovskij the streetcars develop an unheard-of speed.
Kamenoostrovskij: a feather-brained young man with
starch in his only two stone shirts and a sea breeze in
his streetcar-filled head. It is a young dandy out of work,
carrying its houses under its arm like an idle fop returning
with his airy bundle from the laundress.

—Nikolaj Aleksandrovich, Father Bruni![57] Parnok hailed
the clean-shaven priest from Kostroma, obviously not yet
accustomed to his habit, who was carrying in his hand a
savory package of ground, roasted coffee.

—Father Nikolaj Aleksandrovich, walk along with me!
He pulled the priest by his wide lustrine sleeve and led
him along like a small boat. It was difficult to speak with
Father Bruni. Parnok regarded him as, to a certain extent,
a lady.

It was the Kerenskij summer,[58] and the lemonade government was in session.

Everything had been prepared for the grand cotillion.
At one point it appeared as if the citizens would remain
this way forever, like tomcats in turbans.

But the Assyrian bootblacks, like ravens before an eclipse,
were already becoming alarmed, and the dentists began to
run out of false teeth.

I love dentists for their love of art, for their wide horizons,
their tolerance of ideas. Sinner that I am, I love the buzz of
the dentist's drill, that poor earthbound sister of the airplane, which also drills holes with its little bit into the
azure.

Girls were embarrassed in the presence of Father Bruni;
young Father Bruni was embarrassed by trifles of cambric
cloth, but Parnok, covering himself with the authority of
the Church, separate as it was from the government,
squabbled with the proprietress.

It was a frightful time: tailors took back morning coats
and laundresses mocked young men who had lost their
ticket.

The toasted mocha in Father Bruni's sack tickled the nostrils of the furious matron.

They went deeper into the hot cloud of the laundry, where six twittering girls were folding, mangling, and ironing. These crafty seraphim would take a mouthful of water and spray it on the frippery of zephyr and batiste. They played with monstrously heavy irons but did not cease their chatter for a moment. The vaudeville trumpery, spread like foam on long tables, waited its turn. The irons in the red maidenly fingers hissed as they completed their runs. The battleships promenaded along the whipped cream as the girls sprinkled.

Parnok recognized his shirt: it lay on a shelf, glistening with its piqué front, ironed, stuffed with pins, and thinly striped with the color of ripe cherry.

—Girls, whose is that?

—Captain Krzyżanowski's, answered the girls in a lying, unconscionable chorus.

—Father—the proprietress turned to the priest, who stood like some authority in the satiate fog of the laundry, while the steam condensed on his cassock as on a hatrack—Father, if you know this young man, give him some good advice! Even in Warsaw I never saw such a man. Always bringing me work to be done "urgently." He can take his "urgently" and . . . They come walking in here at night from the back way like I was a priest or a midwife . . . I am not fool enough to give him the linen of Captain Krzyżanowski. He's not a policeman, he's a real lieutenant. That gentleman hid for only three days and then the soldiers themselves elected him to the regimental committee and now they carry him above their heads.

No reply could be made to this and Father Bruni turned a pleading glance on Parnok.

And I would have given the girls not irons but Stradivarius violins, light as starling houses, and I would have given each a long scroll of musical notes. All of this cries out to be painted on a ceiling. The cassock in the clouds of steam would pass as the soutane of an abbot directing an orchestra. The six round mouths would open not like holes in bagels from the Petersburg Side[59] but like the astonished little circles in the *Concert at the Pitti Palace.*

···

· IV ·

···

The dentist hung up the snout of the drill and went over to the window.

—Oh-ho. Have a look there!

A crowd was moving along Gorokhovaja Street with a rustle that sounded like a prayer. In the midst of it there had been preserved a free, square-shaped opening. But this air hole, through which shone the wooden paving blocks like chessboard squares, had its own order, its own system: there were to be seen five or six men who appeared to be the masters of ceremony of this whole procession. Their bearing was that of aides-de-camp. Between them were someone's padded shoulders and dandruff-strewn collar. The queen bee of this bizarre hive was the one whom the aides-de-camp were solicitously shoving along, cautiously guiding, and guarding like a pearl.

Could one say that this figure was faceless? No, there was a face, although faces in a crowd have no significance; only napes of necks and ears have an independent life.

Thus advanced the shoulders, like a coat hanger stuffed with wadding, the secondhand jackets, richly bestrewn with dandruff, the irritable napes and dog ears.

—All of those people, Parnok managed to think, are brush salesmen.

Somewhere between the Hay Market and Flour Lane, in the murk of chandlers and tanners, in the wild nursery of dandruff, bedbugs, and protruding ears, was the place that had engendered this strange commotion, spreading nausea and infection.

—They stink of bloated bowels, thought Parnok and was for some reason reminded of the terrible word "entrails." And he felt slightly sick as though from having remembered that an old woman standing near him in a shop recently had asked for "lungs" but in actual fact because of the terrible order which welded that mob together.

Here mutual guarantee was the law: everyone, absolutely everyone, was ready to answer for the preservation and safe delivery of the dandruffy coat hanger to the bank of the Fontanka and the boat with the fish-well. Someone had only to try, with the most modest sort of exclamation, to come to the aid of the owner of the ill-fated collar, which was more highly treasured than sable or marten, and he himself would land in the soup, would be suspect, declared an outlaw and dragged into the empty square. This was the work of that master cooper, Terror.

The citizens (or the napes of their necks), as orderly and ceremonious as Shiahs on the day of Shakhse-Vakse,[60] advanced inexorably toward the Fontanka.

And Parnok spun like a top down the gap-toothed untended stair, leaving the dumbfounded dentist before the sleeping cobra of his drill and displacing any thought by the reiterated words:

"Buttons are made of animal blood."

Time—shy chrysalis, cabbage butterfly sprinkled with flour, young Jewess pressed to the shop window of a watchmaker—you had better not look!

It is not Anatole France whom we are burying in the ostrich-plumed catafalque, high as a poplar, like the pyramid that drives through the night to repair the streetcar poles: we are taking a little man to the Fontanka, to the fish-well boat, to drown him because of an American watch, a conductor's watch of white silver, a lottery watch.

You have had your stroll, my dear fellow, along Shcherbakov Lane, you have spat at the bad Tartar butchershops, hung for a bit on the handrails of a streetcar, taken a trip to see your friend Serëzhka in Gatchina, frequented the public baths and the Ciniselli circus; you have done a bit of living, little man—enough!

First Parnok ran into the watchmaker's, who was sitting like a hunchbacked Spinoza and peering at some springs, like insects under his Jewish magnifying glass.

—Do you have a telephone? I have to warn the police!

But how could a poor Jewish watchmaker on Gorokhovaja Street have a telephone? Daughters he had, melancholy as marzipan dolls, hemorrhoids he had, and tea with lemon, and debts—but no telephone.

Having hastily prepared a cocktail of Rembrandt, of goatish Spanish painting and the chirping of cicadas, and without even having touched this drink with his lips, Parnok dashed off.

Weaving his way sideways along the sidewalk in order to get ahead of the stately procession of lynchers, he ran into one of the mirror shops, which, as everyone knows, are all concentrated on Gorokhovaja. The mirrors threw back and forth the reflections of houses that looked like buffets; the frozen pieces of street, teeming with the beetling mob, appeared in the mirrors still more terrifying and shaggy.

To defend his business, untouched by any shame since 1881, the suspicious Czech proprietor slammed the door in his face.

At the corner of Voznesenskij there appeared Captain Krzyżanowski himself with his pomaded moustache. He was wearing a military topcoat, but with a saber, and was nonchalantly whispering to his lady the sweet nothings of the Horse Guard.

Parnok raced up to him as though he were his best friend and implored him to draw his weapon.

—I respect the moment, the bowlegged captain coldly replied, but pardon me, I am with a lady. And skillfully seizing his companion, he jingled his spurs and disappeared into a cafe.

Parnok ran, tripping along the paving blocks with the little sheep hooves of his patent leather shoes. More than anything in the world he feared to attract upon himself the displeasure of the mob.

There are people who for some reason or other displease mobs. The mob picks them out at once, taunts them, and pulls them by the nose. Children have no special liking for them and women find them unattractive.

Parnok was among this number.

His schoolmates called him "sheep," "patent leather hoof," "Egyptian stamp," and other insulting names. For no earthly reason, the brats had circulated the rumor that he was a "spot remover," that is, that he knew some special preparation which would remove oil spots, ink spots, etc., and for fun they would filch their mothers' shapeless old clothes, bring them to class, and with an innocent expression ask Parnok to "remove this little spot."

And here is the Fontanka—the Undine of rag pickers and hungry students with long, greasy hair; the Lorelei of boiled crawfish, who makes music on a comb with missing teeth; the patroness of the shabby Maly Theater with its seedy, bald Melpomene, like a witch perfumed with patchouli.

Well! The Egyptian Bridge never so much as smelled Egypt, and not a single honest man ever laid eyes on Mr. Kalinkin.[61]

The innumerable swarm of human locusts (God knows where they were coming from) blackened the banks of the Fontanka and clung round the fish-well boat, the barges loaded with cordwood, the wharves, the granite steps, and even the boats of the Ladoga potters. Thousands of eyes gazed into the water with its oily rainbows, flashing with all the hues of kerosene, mother-of-pearl filth, and peacock tails.

Petersburg had declared itself Nero and was as loathsome as if it were eating a soup of crushed flies.

Nevertheless, he telephoned from a pharmacy, telephoned the police, telephoned the government, the state, which had vanished, sleeping like a carp.

He might with equal success have telephoned Proserpine or Persephone, who had not yet had a telephone installed.

Telephones in pharmacies are made of the very finest scarlatina wood. The scarlatina tree grows in enema groves and smells of ink.

Do not telephone from Petersburg pharmacies: the instrument sloughs its skin and the voice fades. Remember that no telephone has yet been installed for Proserpine or Persephone.

My pen sketches a beautiful moustached Greek woman and someone's fox-like chin.

It is thus that arabesques spring up in the margins of first drafts and live independent, gorgeous, and perfidious lives.

Little men shaped like violins drink the milk of the paper.

Here is Babel: the fox chin and paw-like glasses.

Parnok is an Egyptian stamp.

Artur Jakovlevich Hofman—an official in the Greek section of the Ministry of Foreign Affairs.

The French horns of the Mariinskij Theater.

Another moustached Greek woman.

And a blank space for the others.

The swallows of the Hermitage chirped about the sun of Barbizon, about plein-air painting, about coloring like spinach with croutons—in short, about everything that is lacking in the gloomily Flemish Hermitage.

But I shall not receive an invitation to the luncheon of Barbizon even though in my childhood I did tear down the notched, hexagonal lanterns of the coronation and directed toward the sandy pine groves and heather now the irritatingly red trachoma, now the blue noonday cud of some alien planet, now the violet night of a cardinal.

Mother seasoned the salad with egg yolks and sugar.

The torn, crumpled ears of the salad and the marrow died together from vinegar and sugar.

The air, vinegar, and sun were kneaded together with green rags into one complete day of Barbizon, burning with salt, trellises, glass beads, gray leaves, larks, and dragonflies and loud with the sound of crockery.

The Sunday of Barbizon, fanning itself with newspapers and napkins, progressed toward its zenith, lunch, while it scattered the lawn with *feuilletons* and notes about actresses slender as pins.

Guests in wide trousers and leonine velvet vests converged upon the parasols of Barbizon. And women brushed the fruit flies from their round shoulders.

The open wagonettes of the railroad were loath to submit to the steam and, having flapped their curtains, played lotto with the field of camomile.

The top-hatted locomotive with its chicken pistons was outraged at the weight of the chapeaux-claques and muslin.

The barrel sprinkled the street with twine of frail and fragile strings.

The air itself already seemed to be a huge railroad station for the fat, impatient roses.

And brilliant black ants, like the carnivorous actors of the Chinese theater in an old play with an executioner, strutted their turpentine braids and dragged after them the martial sections of a body that had not yet been hacked to pieces as they staggered with their strong, agate rears, like military horses galloping up a hill in farthingales of dust.

Parnok shook himself.

A slice of lemon is a ticket to the fat roses of Sicily, and floor-polishers dance with Egyptian gestures.

The elevator is out of order.

The Menshevik partisans, organizing the night duty at the carriage gates, go from house to house.

Life is both terrifying and beautiful!

He is a lemon seed thrown into a crevice in the granite of Petersburg and will be drunk with black Turkish coffee by the winged night that is approaching.

· V ·

In May Petersburg somehow reminds one of an information booth[62] that does not give out information—especially in the Palace Square area. It is positively terrifying how everything has been prepared for the opening of the historic session: white sheets of paper, sharpened pencils, and a carafe of boiled water.

I repeat once more: the grandeur of this place is that no information is ever given to anyone. At that moment some deaf-mutes were passing through the square: with their hands they were twisting a rapid thread. They were conversing. The senior among them controlled the shuttle. They helped him.

From time to time a boy would run up from one side with his fingers spread so wide that he seemed to be asking for the thread, laced diagonally upon them, to be removed lest it damage the weaving. For all of them together (there were four) it was obviously intended that there be five skeins. There was one skein extra. They were speaking the language of swallows and pan-handlers and, constantly basting up the air with huge stitches, were making a shirt of it.

In a rage the chief tangled all the yarn.

The deaf-mutes disappeared into the General Staff Arch; they went on twisting their yarn, but were already much more tranquil, as if they were releasing messenger pigeons in various directions.

Musical notation caresses the eye no less than music itself soothes the ear. The blacks of the piano scale climb up and down like lamplighters. Each measure is a little boat loaded with raisins and black grapes.

A page of music is, firstly, the deployment in battle of sailing flotillas and, secondly, the plan according to which night, arranged in plum pits, sinks.

The colossal arpeggiated descents in Chopin's mazurkas, the wide staircases festooned with bells in the Liszt études, Mozart's hanging gardens with parterres, trembling on five wires—these have nothing in common with the undersized shrubbery of the Beethoven sonatas.

The mirage cities of musical notation stand like starling houses in boiling pitch.

Schubert's vineyard of notes is always pecked right down to the seeds and lashed by storms.

When hundreds of lamplighters rush about the streets with their little ladders hanging flats on rusty hooks,[63] strengthening the weathervane of sharps, taking down entire placards of stringy measures—that, of course, is Beethoven; but when the cavalry of eights and sixteenths in their paper plumes with horse insignia and little standards throw themselves into the attack—that, too, is Beethoven.

A page of music is a revolution in an ancient German city.

Macrocephalic children. Starlings. They are unhitching the carriage of the prince. Chess players are running out of the coffee houses waving queens and pawns.

There are turtles sticking out their tender heads and competing in a race: that is Handel.

But how warlike are the pages of Bach—those astonishing sheaves of dried mushrooms.

On Sadovaja near the Church of the Intercession stands a fire tower. On freezing January days it throws out alarm signals like grapes—to assemble the brigades. It was not far from there that I studied music. They taught me how to place my hands according to the system of Leszetycki.[64]

Let the languid Schumann hang up notes as if they were linen put out to dry, while downstairs Italians stroll about with their noses in the air; let the most difficult passages of Liszt, waving their crutches about, drag the fire ladder there and back.

The grand piano is an intelligent and good-natured house animal with fibrous, wooden flesh, golden veins, and eternally inflamed bone. We protected it from catching a cold and nourished it with sonatinas, light as asparagus.

Lord! Do not make me like Parnok! Give me the strength to distinguish myself from him.

For I also have stood in that terrifying, patient line which creeps toward the yellow window of the box office—first out in the cold, then under the low, bathhouse ceiling of the vestibule of the Aleksandrinskij Theater. And I am terrified by the theater as by a hut with no chimney, as by a village bathhouse where a bestial murder was committed for the sake of a half-length coat and a pair of felt boots. And I, too, am sustained by Petersburg alone—the Petersburg of concerts, yellow, ominous, sullen, and wintry.

My pen has become insubordinate: it has splintered and squirted its black blood out in all directions, as if it were attached to the desk in the telegraph office, a public pen, ruined by scoundrels in fur coats, having exchanged its swallowy flourish, its original stroke, for such phrases as "Come for God's sake," "Miss you," "kisses," penned by unshaven lechers whispering their little message into their fur collars, warm with their breath.

The kerosene lamp existed before the primus. Mica window and collapsible lighthouse. Like the tower of Pisa the kerosene lamp nodded to Parnok, baring its patriarchal wick and relating in a good-natured way the story of the youths in the fiery furnace.

I am not afraid of incoherence and gaps.

I shear the paper with long scissors.

I paste on ribbons as a fringe.

A manuscript is always a storm, worn to rags, torn by beaks.

It is the first draft of a sonata.

Scribbling is better than writing.

I do not fear seams or the yellowness of the glue.

I am a tailor, I am an idler.

I draw Marat[65] in his stocking.

I draw martins.

In our family the thing that was most feared was "soot"—that is, lampblack from the kerosene lamps. The cry "soot, soot" sounded like "fire, we're on fire," and everyone would run into the room where the lamp was playing tricks. Waving their arms in the air, they would stop and sniff the air, which was filled with a swarm of live, whiskered, fluttering tea leaves.

The guilty lamp was executed by lowering the wick.

Then the little dormer windows would be immediately thrown open and through them would shoot a frost like champagne, hastily chilling the whole room with the moustached butterflies of "soot," settling on the piqué bedspreads and pillowcases like an ether of grippe, a sublimate of pneumonia.

—Don't go in there—the dormer window—whispered mother and grandmother.

But even into the keyhole it forced its way—the forbidden chill, the miraculous guest from diphtherial space.

The Judith of Giorgione slipped away from the eunuchs of the Hermitage.

The trotting horse throws out its pasterns.

Little silver glasses fill up the Millionnaja.

Damned dream! Damned squares of this shameless city!

He made a weak, pleading gesture with his hand, dropped a sheet of perfumed, powdered paper, and sat down on a road marker.

He recalled his inglorious victories, his rendezvous (for which he waited ignominiously in the street), the telephones in beer halls, terrifying as the pincers of a crawfish . . . The numbers of useless, burned-out telephones . . .

The luxurious rattle of a droshky evaporated in a silence that was as suspect as the prayer of a cuirassier.

What is to be done? To whom can one complain? To which seraphim should one deliver the shy, concert-going soul belonging to the raspberry paradise of contrabasses and drones?

Scandal is the name of the demon discovered by Russian prose or by Russian life itself sometime in the forties. It is not catastrophe, though it apes it: a foul transformation by which a dog's head sprouts from a man's shoulders. Scandal carries a soiled, expired passport issued by literature, of which it is the spawn, the beloved offspring. A little grain has disappeared: a homeopathic liqueur bonbon, a tiny dose of a cold, white substance . . . In those distant days when men had recourse to the cuckoo duel—that duel in which the opponents stood in a dark room and fired their pistols into cabinets of chinaware, into inkpots, and family portraits —that little pellet was called "honor."

Once, some bearded literati in trousers as wide as pneumatic bells climbed up on a photographer's starling house and had their picture taken in a splendid daguerrotype. Five of them were sitting, four standing behind the backs of the nut-wood chairs. In front of them in the picture was a little boy in a Circassian coat and a little girl with her hair in ringlets, and darting about between the legs of the company was a cat. He was removed. All their faces expressed one alarmingly grave question: what is the current price of a pound of elephant meat?

That evening in a villa in Pavlovsk these writing gentlemen had raked a poor youngster, Ippolit, over the coals, thus spoiling his chance to finish reading his checkered notebook. Another one trying to be Rousseau!

They did not see and did not understand the charming city with its clean, ship-like lines.

And the imp, scandal, installed itself in an apartment on Razezzhaja Street, having attached a bronze plaque bearing the name of an Attorney at Law—that apartment remains unchanged to this day, like a museum, like the Pushkin House—it snored on the ottomans, stamped about in the entrance hall (people living under the star of scandal never know how to leave on time), made a nuisance of itself with its begging for favors, and said long, tedious goodbyes as it fussed about in someone else's galoshes.

Gentlemen, litterateurs! As ballet slippers belong to ballerinas, so the galoshes—to you. Try them on, exchange them—this is your dance. It is performed in dark antechambers, but on one strict condition: disrespect for the master of the house. Twenty years of such a dance make an epoch, forty—history. That is your right.

Currant smiles of the ballerinas,
muttering of the slippers rubbed with talc, the military complexity and insolent multitude of the string orchestra, hidden in a luminous ditch where the musicians became

confused, like dryads, by the branches, roots, and fiddle-sticks

the vegetable obedience of the corps de ballet,

the splendid disdain for motherhood:

—They've just played sixty-six with this king and queen who don't dance.

—The youthful-looking grandmother of Giselle pours milk around, probably almond milk.

—Every ballet is to a certain extent a serf ballet. No, no, you can't argue with me on this point!

The January calendar with its ballet goats, its model dairy of myriad worlds, its crackle of a deck of cards being unwrapped . . .

Approaching from the rear the indecently waterproof building of the Mariinskij Theater:

—Detectives-scalpers, scalpers-detectives,

Why are you roving around, my dears, in the cold?

Some find a ticket to get in

Others are tricked out of their skin.

—No, no matter what you say, at the basis of the classical ballet there lies a fearful threat—a chunk of the "governmental ice."

—What do you think, where was Anna Karenina sitting?

—Consider: in the ancient world they had amphitheaters, but we, in modern Europe, have tiers. Both in the frescoes of the Last Judgment and at the Opera. One and the same world view.

The streets, smoky with bonfires, whirled like a carousel.

—Driver, to "Giselle"—that is, to the Mariinskij!

The Petersburg cabby is a myth, a Capricorn. He should be put in the zodiac. There he would not be lost with his old woman's purse, his sleigh runners, narrow as truth, and his oaty voice.

The droshky had a classic chic, rather Muscovite than Petersburg; with its high-riding body, its brilliantly polished fenders, and its tires inflated to the limit of possibility, it could not have looked more like a Greek chariot.

Captain Krzyżanowski whispered into the criminal, pink little ear:

—Don't worry about him. My word of honor, he is having a tooth filled. I will tell you what's more: this morning on the Fontanka he—I don't know which—either stole a watch or had one stolen from him. The scoundrel! A filthy story!

The white night, having stridden through Kolpina and Srednjaja Rogatka, arrived at Tsarskoe Selo. The palaces stood about, white with fright, like silken cowls. At times their whiteness resembled a shawl of Orenburg down, washed with soap and alkali. In the deep green foliage bicycles buzzed—the metal hornets of the park.

Any further whiteness was unthinkable; one minute more, it seemed, and the entire hallucination would break into pieces like fresh bonnyclabber.

A terrifying stone lady "in the high boots of Peter the Great" walks about the streets and speaks.

—Garbage in the squares . . . Simoom . . . Arabs . . . "Semën simpered to the proseminar."[66]

Petersburg, you are responsible for your poor son!

For all this melee, for this pitiful love of music, for every gram of those liqueur bonbons, carried in a paper sack by the girl student sitting in the gallery of the Nobility Hall, you, Petersburg, will answer!

Memory is a sick Jewish girl who steals away in the night from her parents' house to the Nicholas Station thinking that perhaps someone will turn up to carry her off.

The "little old insurance man," Geshka Rabinovich, as soon as he was born, had asked for some policy forms and Ralle soap. He lived on the Nevskij in a tiny, girlish apartment. Everyone was touched by his illicit liaison with a certain Lizochka.—Genrikh Jakovlevich is asleep, Lizochka would say, putting her finger to her lips and blushing all over. She hoped, of course (insane hope) that Genrikh Jakovlevich would still grow a bit and would live long years with her, and that their rosy, childless marriage, consecrated by the archbishops of Filippov's coffee house, was only the beginning . . .

But Genrikh Jakovlevich, with the bounciness of a toy dog, ran up and down stairs insuring what remained of people's lives.

In Jewish apartments there reigns a melancholy, be-whiskered silence.

It is composed of the conversations between the pendulum and the bread crumbs on the checkered tablecloth and the silver glass holders.

Aunt Vera would come to dinner and bring along her father, old Pergament. Behind Aunt Vera's shoulders there stood the myth of the ruin of Pergament. He had an apartment of forty rooms on the Kreshchatik in Kiev. "A house is a full cup."[67] On the street beneath the forty rooms beat the hooves of Pergament's horses. Pergament himself "clipped coupons."

Aunt Vera was a Lutheran and sang with the parishioners in the red church on the Mojka. She exuded the chill of a companion, reader, and hospital nurse—that strange breed of people inimically bound to someone else's life. Her thin Lutheran lips disapproved of the manner in which our household was run and her spinsterish curls hung above the chicken soup with a faint air of disgust.

On appearing at the house, Aunt Vera would merchanically begin to sympathize and offer her Red Cross services as though she were unrolling a spool of gauze and throwing out a streamer of invisible bandage.

The cabriolets drove along the hard pavement of the highway and the men's Sunday coats bristled like roofing iron. The cabriolets drove from *jarvi* to *jarvi*[68] so that the kilometers spilled out like peas and smelled of spirits and cottage cheese. The cabriolets drove, twenty-one and four more, carrying old women in black kerchiefs and in cloth skirts that were stiff as tin. They had to sing songs in the rooster-topped church, drink coffee spiked with pure alcohol, and return by the same road.

The young raven puffed himself up: Welcome to our funeral.

—That's not the way to invite people, twittered the little sparrow in the park of Mon Repos.[69]

Then the lean ravens with feathers that were hard and blue from age interposed: Karl and Amalia Blomquist announce to their family and friends the death of their beloved daughter Elza.

—That is something else again, twittered the little sparrow in the park of Mon Repos.

Boys on the street were fitted out like knights at a tourney: gaiters, wide padded trousers, and ear flaps. The ear flaps caused a buzzing in the head and deafness. In order to answer someone it was necessary to undo the laces that cut into one's chin.

He whirled about in his heavy winter armor like a deaf little knight, not hearing his own voice.

The first isolation from people and from himself and—

who knows?—the sweet adumbration of sclerosis in his
blood (for the time being still rubbed by the shaggy towel
of the seventh year of life)—all this was brought to life
in his ear flaps; and the six-year-old padded Beethoven in
gaiters, armed with his deafness, was pushed out onto the
stairs.

He wanted to turn around and shout, "The scullery maid
is deaf as a spade."

They walked pompously along Ofitserskaja, stopping in
the store to pick out a duchess pear.

Once they dropped in to Aboling's lamp store on
Voznesenskij, where the showy lamps thronged like idiot
giraffes in red hats with festoons and flounces. Here for the
first time they were overcome by the impression of grandeur
and "the forest of things."

They never dropped in to Ejlers' flower shop.[70]

Somewhere the woman doctor Strashuner was practicing.

· VII ·

When a tailor delivers his finished work, you would
never say that he had new clothes on his arm. He somehow
resembles a member of a burial society hastening with the
appurtenances of the ritual to a house marked by Azrail.
Thus the tailor Mervis. Parnok's morning coat did not
warm itself on his hanger long—about two hours; that was
all the time it had to breathe its native caraway air. The
wife of Mervis congratulated him on his success.

—That is nothing, answered the master, flattered. My
grandfather used to say that a real tailor is one who, in
broad daylight, on Nevskij Prospekt, can take a frock coat
off a customer who won't pay.

Then he took the morning coat down from the hanger, blew on it as if it were a cup of hot tea, wrapped it up in a clean linen sheet, and carried it in its white shroud and black calico to Captain Krzyżanowski.

I must confess that I love Mervis—I love his blind face, furrowed by wrinkles that see. Theoreticians of the classical ballet devote great attention to a ballerina's smile; they regard it as an accessory to her movement, an interpretation of her leap, her flight. But sometimes a lowered lid sees more than an eye, and the tiers of wrinkles on a human face peer like a gathering of blind men.

The tailor, then, elegant as porcelain, sweeps along like a convict torn from his plank bed, beaten up by his comrades, like an overheated bath attendant, like a thief in a bazaar, ready to shout his last irresistibly convincing word.

In my perception of Mervis certain images gleam through: a Greek satyr, the unhappy singer Kifared,[71] at times the mask of an actor in a play by Euripides, at times the naked breast and sweaty body of a flogged convict, of an inmate in a Russian flop house, of an epileptic.

I hasten to tell the real truth, I am in a hurry. The word, like aspirin powder, leaves a brassy taste in the mouth.

Cod-liver oil is a mixture of conflagrations and yellow winter mornings, and whale oil has the taste of torn-out eyes that have burst, the taste of revulsion brought to the point of ecstasy.

A bird's eye, suffused with blood, also has its own way of seeing the world.

Books melt like chunks of ice brought into a room. Everything grows smaller. Everything seems to me a book. Where is the difference between a book and a thing? I do not know life: they switched it on me as long ago as the time when I recognized the crunch of arsenic between the teeth of the amorous French brunette, the younger sister of our proud Anna.

Everything grows smaller. Everything melts. Even Goethe melts. Brief is the time allotted us. As it slips away, the hilt of that bloodless, brittle sword, broken off the drainpipe one freezing day, chills the palm.

But thought—like the hangman steel of the "Nurmis"[72] skates, which once skimmed along the blue, pimply ice— has not been blunted.

Thus skates screwed onto shapeless children's shoes, to American laced hooves, grow together with them—lancets of freshness and youth—and the shoes thus equipped, having borne their joyous weight, are transformed into the magnificent remains of a dragon, for which there is neither name nor price.

It is more and more difficult to turn the pages of the frozen book, bound in axes by the light of gas lanterns.

You, wood yards—black libraries of the city—we shall yet read, we shall still have a look.

Somewhere on Podjacheskaja was situated that renowned library whence packs of little brown volumes by Russian and foreign authors (their contagious pages so read that they seemed made of silk) were taken away to the villa. Homely young ladies chose the books from the shelves. For one Bourget, for another Georges Ohnet, for a third something else from the literary lumber room.

Across the street was a fire brigade with hermetically sealed gates and a bell in a mushroom hat.

Some pages were transparent as onion skin.

They were inhabited by measles, scarlatina, and chicken pox.

In the spines of those villa books, often forgotten on the beach, the golden dandruff of the sand had become embedded; no matter how one shook it, it appeared again.

Sometimes out would fall a piece of fern—a little Gothic fir tree, flattened and spoiled—and occasionally the mummy of some nameless northern flower.

Conflagrations and books: that is good.

We shall still see, we shall read.

"Several minutes before the beginning of the agony, a fire brigade thundered along the Nevskij. Everyone dashed to the square, sweaty windows, and Angiolina Bosio— from Piemonte, the daughter of a poor strolling player, *basso comico*—was left for a moment to herself.

The martial trills and cadenzas of the firemen's crowing horns, like the unheard-of gusto of an unconditionally victorious misfortune, forced their way into the stuffy bedroom of the Demidov house. The fire horses with their barrels, carts, and ladders thundered off and the flame of the torches licked the mirrors. But in the guttering consciousness of the dying singer this bedlam of feverish, official clamor, this lunatic gallop in sheepskin coats and helmets, this armful of noises, arrested and driven off under guard, was changed into the appeal of an orchestral overture. In her small homely ears she plainly heard the final measures of the overture to *I due Foscari*, the opera of her London debut . . .

She raised herself a bit and sang what was required, but not in that sweet voice, metallic and pliant, which had made her fame and which the newspapers had praised, but with the chesty, unpracticed timbre of a fifteen-year-old girl, with an incorrect, wasteful production of the sound, for which Professor Cattaneo had been so cross with her.

Farewell Traviata, Rosina, Zerlina . . ."[73]

That evening Parnok did not return home to have dinner and drink tea with the little cakes which he loved like a canary. He listened to the sputter of the blowtorches as they approached the streetcar tracks with their blindingly white, shaggy roses. He received back all the streets and squares of Petersburg in the form of rough galley proofs, he composed the prospects, stitched the gardens.

He approached the raised drawbridges, which reminded him that all must come to an abrupt end, that desolation and the abyss are splendid wares, that there would be, would surely be a leavetaking, that the treacherous levers controlled masses and years.

He waited while on one side and the other the camps of the drivers and pedestrians accumulated like two hostile tribes or generations, quarrelling over the wooden stone-bound book, the interior of which had been ripped out.

He thought of Petersburg as his infantile disease—one had only to regain consciousness, to come to, and the hallucination would vanish: he would recover, become like all other people, even—perhaps—get married. . . . Then no one would dare call him "young man." And he would be through with kissing ladies' hands. They'd had their share! Setting up their own Trianon, damn them! Let some slut, some old bag, some shabby feline stick her paw out to his lips and, by the force of long habit, he would give it a smack! Enough! It was time to put an end to his lap-dog youth. Besides, had not Artur Jakovlevich Hofman promised to find him a place as dragoman, even if only in Greece? And there he would see. He would have himself a new morning coat made, he would have it out with Captain Krzyżanowski, he would show him.

There was only one thing wrong—he had no pedigree. And nowhere to get one. He simply didn't have one and that was all there was to it! Of relatives he had only one, an aunt, Aunt Johanna. A dwarf. A veritable Empress Anna Leopol'dovna. Spoke Russian like God knows what. As if Biron were her blood brother. Little short arms. She couldn't button anything by herself. And she had a maid, Annushka[74]—Psyche.

Yes, with such relatives one could not go far. But—wait a moment—how is that not a pedigree? How not? It is. What about Captain Goljadkin? And the collegiate assessors, to whom "the Lord God might have given more brains and money"?[75] All those people who were shown down the stairs, publicly disgraced, insulted in the forties and fifties of the last century, all those mutterers, windbags in capes, with gloves that had been laundered to shreds, all those who do not "live" but "reside" on Sadovaja and Podjacheskaja in houses made of stale sections of petrified chocolate and grumble to themselves: "How is that possible? Not a penny to my name, and me with a university education?"

One has only to remove the film from the Petersburg air and then its hidden stratum will be laid bare. Under the swan's-down, the eider down, the far end of Gagárin, under the Tuchkov puffs of clouds, under the French *bouchées* of the dying quays, under the little plate-glass windows in the apartments of noblemen and yes-men, there will be revealed something completely unexpected.[76]

But the pen that removes this film is like a doctor's teaspoon—contaminated with a touch of diphtheria. It is better not to touch it.

The mosquito whined:

—Look what has happened to me: I am the last Egyptian —a sober, sober tutor, simple soldier—I am a little bow-legged prince—a beggarly, blood-sucking Ramses—in the north I have become nothing—so little is left of me—I beg your pardon!

—I am the prince of ill fortune—a collegiate assessor of the city of Thebes . . . Everything is the same—not a whit changed—Oh! I am frightened here—Excuse me . . . I am a trifle—I am nothing. I will ask the choleric granite for a kopeck's worth of Egyptian pap, for a kopeck's worth of girl's neck.

—I—don't worry—I'll pay—Excuse me.

To calm himself, he consulted a certain small, unwritten dictionary—or rather, a register of little homey words that had gone out of use. He had long ago composed it in his mind for use in case of misfortune and shock:

"Horseshoe." That was the name for a poppy-seed roll.

"Fromuga"—his mother's name for the large, hinged dormer window, which slammed shut like the lid of a grand piano.

"Don't botch it." This was said about life.

"Do not command." One of the commandments.

These words will suffice to impart the flavor. He accustomed himself to the aroma of this little pinch of them. The past became overwhelmingly real and tickled his nostrils like a shipment of fresh Kjakhta teas.

Carriages drove across the snowy field. Above the field hung a low, police-linen sky which doled out in a miserly way the yellow and, for some reason, shameful light.

I was attached to someone else's family and carriage. A young Jew was counting some new hundred-rouble notes that crackled with a wintry sound.

—Where are we going? I asked an old woman in a gypsy shawl.

—To the city of Malinov, she replied, but with such aching melancholy that my heart contracted with an evil fore boding.

The old woman, rummaging about in her striped bundle, took out some table silver, a cloth, and velvet slippers.

The threadbare wedding carriages crawled on and on, reeling like contrabasses.

In the carriage rode Abrasha Kopeljanskij, with his angina pectoris, Aunt Johanna, rabbis, and photographers. An old music teacher held on his knees a mute keyboard. Wrapped tight in the skirts of the old man's beaver coat was a fidgety rooster destined for ritual Jewish slaughter.

—Look, exclaimed someone, sticking his head out of the window. There is Malinov already.

But there was no city there. Instead, growing right in the snow were some large, warty raspberries.

—But that's a raspberry patch,[77] I gasped, beside myself with joy, and began to run with the others, filling my shoes with snow. My shoe became untied and because of that I was seized with a feeling of great guilt and disorder.

And they led me into a hateful Warsaw room and made me drink water and eat onion.

I kept bending over to tie my shoe with a double knot and put everything in its proper order—but in vain. It was impossible to recoup anything or repair anything: everything went backwards, as always happens in a dream. I scattered the featherbeds of others and ran out into the Taurid Gardens, clasping the favorite plaything of my childhood, an empty candlestick richly covered with stearin, and removed its white bark, tender as a bridal veil.

It is terrifying to think that our life is a tale without a plot or hero, made up out of desolation and glass, out of the feverish babble of constant digressions, out of the delirium of the Petersburg influenza.

Rosy-fingered Dawn has broken her colored pencils. Now they lie scattered about like nestlings with empty, gaping beaks. Meanwhile, I seem to see in absolutely everything the advance deposit of my dear prosaic delirium.

Are you familiar with this condition? When it's just as if every object were running a fever, when they are all joy· ously excited and ill: barriers in the street, posters shedding their skin, grand pianos thronging at the depot like an intelligent, leaderless herd, born for frenzies of the sonata and for boiled water . . .

Then, I confess, I am unable to endure the quarantine and, smashing thermometers, through the contagious labyrinth I boldly stride, behung with subordinate clauses like happy bargain buys . . . and into the waiting sack fly the crisp pastry birds, naive as the plastic art of the first centuries of Christianity, and the *kalatch*, the common *kalatch*, no longer conceals from me that it was conceived by the baker as a Russian lyre of voiceless dough.

The Nevskij in '17: a squadron of Cossacks with their blue caps cocked on their heads, their faces turned in the direction of the sun's path like identical, oblique fifty-kopeck pieces.

Even with one's eyes shut tight, one can tell that those are cavalrymen singing.

The song rocks in the saddles like tremendous free sacks filled with the gold foil of hops.

It is the free victual served with the little trot, jingle, and sweat.

It floats along on blind, shaggy Bashkirs at the level of the plate-glass windows of the first floor as if the very squadron itself were floating on a diaphragm, trusting it more than saddle girths and legs.

Destroy your manuscript, but save whatever you have inscribed in the margin out of boredom, out of helplessness, and, as it were, in a dream. These secondary and involuntary creations of your fantasy will not be lost in the world but will take their places behind shadowy music stands, like third violins at the Mariinskij Theater, and out of gratitude to their author strike up the overture to *Lenore* or the *Egmont* of Beethoven.

What a pleasure for the narrator to switch from the third person to the first! It is just as if, after having had to drink from tiny inconvenient thimble-sized glasses, one were suddenly to say the hell with them, to get hold of oneself, and drink cold, unboiled water straight out of the faucet.

Terror takes me by the hand and leads me. A white cotton glove. A woman's glove without fingers. I love terror, I respect it. I almost said "With it, I'm not terrified!" Mathematicians should have built a tent for terror, for it is the coordinate of time and space: they participate in it like the rolled-up felt in the nomad tent of the Kirgiz. Terror unharnesses the horses when one has to drive and sends us dreams with unnecessarily low ceilings.

At the beck and call of my consciousness are two or three little words: "and there," "already," "suddenly"; they rush about from car to car on the dimly lighted Sevastopol train, halting on the platforms where two thundering frying pans hurl themselves at one another and crawl apart.

The railroad has changed the whole course, the whole structure, the whole rhythm of our prose. It has delivered it over to the senseless muttering of the French *moujik* out of *Anna Karenina*. Railroad prose, like the woman's purse of that ominous *moujik*, is full of the coupler's tools, delirious particles, grappling-iron prepositions, and belongs rather among things submitted in legal evidence: it is divorced from any concern with beauty and that which is beautifully rounded.

Yes, it is there where the beefy levers of locomotives are covered in hot oil that this dear little prose breathes, stretched out at its full length; it is there that it measures, shameless thing that it is, and winds on its own fraudulent yardstick the six hundred and nine versts of the Nikolaevskij road, with its sweating carafes of vodka.

At 9:30 p.m. the former Captain Krzyżanowski was planning to board the Moscow express. He had packed in his suitcase Parnok's morning coat and best shirts. The morning coat, having tucked in its fins, fit into the suitcase especially well, almost without a wrinkle, like a frolicsome dolphin of cheviot, to which it was related by its cut and by its youthful soul.

At Ljuban' and Bologoe Captain Krzyżanowski came out to drink some vodka and kept repeating "soiré moiré, poiré" or God knows what other officer's nonsense. He even tried to have a shave in the car, but in that he did not succeed.

At Klin he tried a cup of railroad coffee, the recipe for which has not changed since the days of Anna Karenina: chicory, with a slight admixture of cemetery earth or some other kind of nastiness like that.

In Moscow he stopped at the Hotel Select—an excellent hotel on Malaja Lubjanka—where he was given a room that had formerly been used as a store; in place of a regular window it had a fashionable shop window, heated by the sun to an improbable degree.

NOTES TO THE PROSE

The Noise of Time

1. *Gluxie gody*: The word *gluxoj* is rich in emotional associations and therefore virtually untranslatable. It has the primary meaning "deaf," but it also can mean "overgrown, wild; dead (of a season); suppressed, obscure, smouldering; remote, out of the way, god-forsaken" and so on. The phrase *gluxie gody* has, moreover, literary associations, since it recalls the poem by Aleksandr Blok which begins

> Roždënnye v goda gluxie
> Puti ne pomnjat svoego

[Those born in remote and desolate years do not remember their own path.] (*Sobranie sočinenij* [Collected Works], III [Moscow, 1960], 278.) It is characteristic of Mandel'štam's relationship to Blok that he summons up the older poet only to contradict him.

2. "Near the station is the large railway restaurant of Vauxhall . . . ; popular concerts with a good band every evening in summer (adm. free; reserved seats 10-50 cop.)" (Baedeker's *Russia* [1914], p. 189.)

3. Nikolaj Vladimirovič Galkin (1856-1906), violinist, conductor, teacher. Between 1892-1903 Galkin conducted weekly concerts in Pavlovsk, where the works of Russian composers were often given their first performance.

4. Nikolaj Nikolaevič Figner (1857-1918), tenor, soloist at the Mariinskij from 1887-1907.

5. Gostinyj Dvor: "The Gostinyj Dvor, or Bazaar. . . , bounded on the E. by the Sadovaja and on the S. by the Černyšov Pereulok, is an extensive building painted white and enclosing several courts. It was erected in 1761-85 by Vallin de la Mothe and completely rebuilt at the end of the 19th century. The arcades on the ground floor and the first floor contain about 200 shops, which, however, are less elegant than the other shops on the Nevskij." (Baedeker's *Russia* [1914], p. 104f.) The building still stands, bears the same name, and serves the same function in present-day Leningrad.

6. Engineers' Palace: "To the E. of the Mixajlovskij Garden lies the Engineers' Palace, or Old Michael Palace. . . , built in a

mediaeval style in the reign of Paul I. between 1797 and 1800. . . . In 1822 the building was fitted up as an Engineering Academy (Nikolaevskaja inženernaja akademija)." (Baedeker, 118)

7. bullet-riddled banners: "On the pillars and walls are 103 banners and eagles captured from Napoleon, which give the church a military aspect." (Baedeker, 104)

8. Andrej Ivanovič Željabov (1850-1881) was the founder of the People's Will, a group of revolutionaries responsible for the assassination of Alexander II. Sof'ja L'vovna Perovskaja (1853-1881) was an adherent. Both were executed.

9. bathing houses: Wooden structures built in the water for the shelter of modest swimmers.

10. Narodnyj Dom: literally, People's House. Its full name was Narodnyj dom Imperatora Nikolaja II [People's House of Czar Nicholas II]. Located in the Alexander Park, on the north and east sides of the Kronwerk Canal, it contained a large theater of 4,000 seats. This was the most famous of a number of institutions with the name Narodnyj Dom in pre-revolutionary Russia which served as combined cultural and recreation centers.

11. Jewish quarter: This was the Kolomna District, which Baedeker treats in two brief paragraphs of reduced type and dismisses as "unattractive" (p. 124). The Litovskij (or Lithuanian) Castle was in fact the city prison.

12. Covetous Knight: The title and principal character of one of the little tragedies of Aleksandr Pushkin.

13. hares: This was the term for illegal passengers on streetcars, trains, and other forms of public transportation. It probably derives from their leaping on and off the moving vehicle between stops to avoid paying.

14. "Dubbeln, the oldest of the Riga bathing resorts, is (like Majorenhof) very noisy; among the visitors are many Jews." (Baedeker, 64)

15. sound recording device: *zvukopriëmnik*. I am not sure of this meaning. Mr. Alfred J. Swan (author of *Scriabin*, London, 1923) informs me that it could not, as might be thought, be an error for the *clavier à lumière*, a huge reflector used for casting colored lights over the hall to the accompaniment of

the music, since this innovation of Scriabin's *Prometheus* was never used at any performance that Mandel'štam could have witnessed.

16. Josef Casimir Hofmann (1876-1957). Jan Kubelik (1880-1940).

17. Hôtel d'Europe: At the time of which Mandel'štam writes, the Evropejskaja Gostinica, which is now one of the Intourist hotels in Leningrad, was known even to Russians by its French name.

18. Count Sergej Jul'evič Vitte [Witte] (1849-1915), Minister of Finance 1892-1903, Prime Minister 1903-1906.

19. Pëtr Isaevič Vejnberg [Weinberg] (1831-1908), a Russian poet and translator. Mandel'štam for some reason reverses his first name and patronymic, making it Isaj Petrovič.

20. Maksim Maksimovič Kovalevskij (1851-1916), professor of constitutional law and from 1909 to his death editor of the journal *Vestnik Evropy* [Messenger of Europe]. Ivan Il'ič Petrunkevič (1844-1928), a founder of the Constitutional Democratic Party and, from 1907, publisher of *Reč'* [Speech] and *Sovremennyj Mir* [The Contemporary World].

21. Fëdor Izmajlovič Rodičev (1856-1933), a leader and the principal spokesman of the Constitutional Democratic Party. Nikolaj Fëdorovič Annenskij (1843-1912), editor of *Russkoe Bogatstvo* [Russian Wealth] and a founder of the People's Socialist Party. Fëdor Dmitrievič Batjuškov (1857-1920), literary historian and critic, privatdocent in the University of St. Petersburg and editor of *Mir Božij* [God's World] from 1902-1906. Dmitrij Nikolaevič Ovsjaniko-Kulikovskij (1853-1920), editor of a well-known history of Russian literature and one of the editors of *Vestnik Evropy*.

22. Vladimir Nabokov (b. 1899), the author of *Lolita* and other novels and the translator of Pushkin's *Eugene Onegin*, attended the Tenishev School some ten years after Mandel'štam. He was driven to school in a limousine by a liveried chauffeur and presumably belonged to the "military, privileged, almost aristocratic undercurrent." Nabokov's memoirs in *Speak, Memory* (New York, 1947; original title, *Conclusive Evidence*), published in a Russian version as *Drugie berega* [Other Shores],

(New York, 1954), provide a fascinatingly different slant on this remarkable institution.

23. Mixail Matveevič Stasjulevič (1826-1911), professor of history in St. Petersburg and one of the founders of the Party for Democratic Reforms. From 1866 to 1908 he was editor and publisher of *Vestnik Evropy* [Messenger of Europe].

24. luminous personality: *svetlaja ličnost'*. Also on p. 84.

25. SR: Socialist Revolutionary, a political party formed in 1902 by various factions of the Populists. SD: Social Democratic (or, to give it the full title, Russian Social Democratic Labor Party), founded in 1898, was split in 1903 into two factions, the Mensheviks and Bolsheviks.

26. V.V.G.: Vladimir Vasil'evič Gippius (1876-1941). An early Symbolist poet and Mandel'štam's teacher in the Tenishev School, of which he was at one time director (see Chap. 14). He was the author of *Puškin i xristianstvo* [Pushkin and Christianity] (Petersburg, 1915) and wrote poetry under the pseudonyms V. Bestužev and V. Neledinskij. Memoirs of him can be found in Valerij Brjusov's *Dnevniki 1891-1910* [Journals] (Moscow, 1927).

27. chicken legs: A reference to line 11 of the prologue to Pushkin's *Ruslan and Ljudmila*: "Izbuška tam na kur'ix nož-kax" [A hut (stands) there on chicken legs].

28. Viktor Mixajlovič Černov (1873-1952), a leader of the SR party and a disciple of Mixajlovskij. Nikolaj Konstantinovič Mixajlovskij (1842-1904), a leading literary critic and principal ideologist of Populism. Pëtr Lavrovič Lavrov (1823-1900), a leading Populist philosopher, wrote his major work, the *Historical Letters* (1868-1869), under the pseudonym of P. L. Mirtov.

29. Konevskoj: Ivan Ivanovič Oreus (1877-1901), an early and now forgotten Symbolist, wrote under the name of I. Konevskoj.

30. Aleksej Vasil'evič Pešexonov (1867-1933), a leader of the People's Socialist Party, formed in 1906 from the ranks of the right SR's. Venedikt Aleksandrovič Mjakotin (1867-1937). Mark Andreevič Natanson (1850-1919).

31. Lev Maksimovič Klejnbort [Kleinbort] (1875-1938), the editor of *Temy žizni* [Themes of Life], a weekly published in St. Petersburg in 1906-1907, and the author of *Očerki*

narodnoj literatury [Studies in the Literature of the People], (Leningrad, 1924). His real name was Lev Naumovič Klejnbort.

32. Franz Stuck (1863-1928), a German artist. The small satirical and grotesque sculptures of Innokentij Žukov depicted human sloth, pride, and so on, and were widely reproduced on postcards and elsewhere.

33. P. Ja.: Pëtr Filippovič Jakubovič (pseudo. L. Mel'šin) (1860-1911), a poet and revolutionary associated with the People's Will party. Mixail Larionovič Mixajlov (1826-1865), revolutionary poet best known for his verse translations. Evgenij Mixailovič Tarasov (b. 1882), a revolutionary poet who gave up writing in 1909 and devoted himself thereafter to economics.

34. thick reviews: *tolstye žurnaly*, a term used of all the leading monthlies such as *Vestnik Evropy, Russkoe Bogatstvo*, etc.

35. According to Anna Axmatova's memoir in *Vozdušnye Puti* [Aerial Ways] IV (1965), 24, it was to Mandel'štam himself that this remark was made by the owner of the print shop where *Kamen'* [Stone] was published.

36. fighting organization: A semi-independent group within the SR party having as its function the commission of acts of terror against members of the government. It was led by the notorious Evno Fišelevič Azef (1869-1918), who proved to be a double agent.

37. Grigorij Aleksandrovič Geršuni (1870-1908). A revolutionary terrorist among the SR's, organizer of the "fighting organization" later led by Azef.

38. Vera Fëdorovna Komissarževskaja (1864-1910).

39. *raznočinec*: An intellectual associated with none of the principal social classes, such as the nobility, priesthood, merchants, etc.

40. Gippius: See note 26 above.

41. Konevskoj: See note 29 above. Aleksandr Mixajlovič Dobroljubov (1876-1944[?]). An early Symbolist poet, D. soon combined his poetry with religious fervor, became the leader of a small sect, and vanished "into the people."

42. Konevic (formerly Konevec), a large island in Lake Ladoga and the subject of a poem (1898) by Ivan Konevskoj.

43. Its house was a full cup: A Russian adage signifying abundance and plenty. It occurs again on p. 177, below.

44. Walsingham: A character in Pushkin's *Feast During the Plague*, translated from a scene in John Wilson's dramatic poem *The City of the Plague*.

Theodosia

45. Centrosojuz: Central'nyj sojuz potrebitel'skix obščestv [Central Union of Consumers' Cooperatives].

46. Mixail Vasil'evič Mabo (1878-1961), a director of the Azov Bank, left the Soviet Union in 1921. I had the pleasure of an interview with him in Freehold, New Jersey, where he was living in retirement, a few weeks before his death in 1961. Mabo (or Mabo-Azovskij, to use his nom de plume) recorded some of his recollections of Mandel'štam in an article in the *Novoe Russkoe Slovo* (New York) for 14 January 1949. Perhaps it should be noted that Mabo remembers Aleksandr Sarandinaki to have been Harbor Master in Kerč', not in Feodosija, where the post was filled by a certain A. Novinskij. And, to fulfill a pledge made to Mabo, I should like to record that he did not write poems, as Mandel'štam says, but plays, and he was still writing them at the time of his death.

47. bobbies: Mandel'štam's error for "tommies."

48. railroad birds: I am trying to suggest Mandel'štam's pun on the resemblance between *kurjane* [residents of Kursk] and *kury* [chickens], which accounts for the image of their being taken down from a roost.

49. The Royal Mantle of the Law: *Barmy zakona*. I take the English translation of this term from Vjačeslav Zavališin's *Early Soviet Writers* (New York, 1958), p. 55.

50. OSVAG: *Osvedomitel'noe agentstvo*, the information and propaganda section of the White Army.

51. *sotnik*: A Cossack military rank (equivalent to lieutenant in the Russian army); originally, a commander of a unit of 100 men.

The Egyptian Stamp

52. Giacomo Guarenghi (1744-1817), one of the number of great Italian architects who built the most beautiful buildings in St. Petersburg and its environs.

53. *Kreščatik*: the name of the main street of Kiev. *ščastie*: "happiness." Mandel'štam gives the pronunciation rather than the spelling, which is *sčast'e. ščavel'*: "sorrel."

54. Lucien Chardon de Rubempré is a character in Balzac's *Illusions perdues* and *Splendeurs et misères des courtisanes*.

55. Alberto Santos-Dumont (1873-1932), Brazilian airship pioneer.

56. Sands: the popular and unofficial name for a section of St. Petersburg that lay roughly at the juncture of the Litejnaja and Roždestvenskaja quarters.

57. Nikolaj Aleksandrovič Bruni: See p. 47.

58. Kerenskij summer: The summer between the February and October revolutions of 1917; from Aleksandr Fëdorovič Kerenskij (b. 1881), the president of the Provisional Government.

59. Petersburg Side: The *Peterburgskaja storona* is the oldest quarter of the city, comprising the several islands between the Neva and the Bol'šaja Nevka. It contains the Fortress of SS. Peter and Paul.

60. The Shiahs (or Shiites) constitute one of the two principal religious sects of Islam. The feastday, more commonly spelled Šaxsej-Vaxsej and identical with the Ashura of English usage, commemorates the sufferings of the descendants of Ali who were killed in the Battle of Karbala in 680. Here, from a source which has a certain piquant appropriateness (see p. 47), is a further comment on this feast: "Aujourd'hui, pendant une fête musulmane, les Persans se portent eux-mêmes des coups de poignard et se réjouissent à la vue de leur sang qui coule à la gloire de leur dévotion. Cette coutume masochiste, connue sous le nom de Chakhsé-Vakhsé, persiste encore au Caucase." (Valentin Parnac, *Histoire de la danse* [Paris, 1932], p. 17.)

61. Kalinkin: the name of a bridge across the Fontanka.

62. information booth: *adresnyj stol*—as in Leningrad today, a booth for obtaining addresses and telephone numbers. No general directory of private telephones is published.

63. hooks: *krjuki*, which can also refer to musical signs in ancient Russian notation.

64. Teodor Leszetycki (1830-1915).

65. The name "Marat" is suggested by the verb *marat'* [scribble], three lines above.

66. *Prosemenil Semën v proseminarij.* Said by the students in the Puškin seminar at the University of St. Petersburg about their professor, Semën Afanas'evič Vengerov, Mandel'štam's relative, in reference to his mincing gait (see pp. 61, 85). See Boris Ejxenbaum, *Moj vremennik* [My Journal], Leningrad, 1929, p. 38.

67. "A house is a full cup." See note 43 above.

68. *järvi*: the Finnish word for lake.

69. Mon Repos: The country seat of Baron von Nikolai, said by Baedeker (207) to be "the finest point in the environs of Viborg."

70. Ejlers' flower shop: See p. 45f.

71. Kifared: The reference is to Innokentij Annenskij's tragedy *Famira Kifared* (1913), based on the myth of Thamyras, whose playing on the cythara was so accomplished that he challenged the Muses themselves to a contest and, defeated, was deprived of both his talent and his eyesight.

72. Nurmis: so in Mandel'štam's text, though it is probably an error for the name of Paavo Johannes Nurmi (b. 1897), the great Finnish athlete.

73. Angiolina Bosio (1830-1859, according to *Grove's Dictionary of Music and Musicians* [London, 1954]), an Italian soprano, sang in the capitals of Europe, in America, and for four seasons, beginning in 1856, in the opera in St. Petersburg. She died in St. Petersburg 13 April 1859 of pneumonia and was buried in the Catholic cemetery there. It is worth noting that the death of Angiolina Bosio was also the subject of four of the most beautiful lines of the poet Nikolaj Nekrasov:

> Vspomnim Bozio. Čvannyj Petropol'
> Ne žalel ničego dlja neë,
> No naprasno ty kutala v sobol'
> Solov'inoe gorlo svoë.

[Let us remember Bosio. Arrogant Petropolis spared no pains on her behalf. But it was in vain that you wrapped your nightingale throat in sable.] This is from the poem "O pogode"

[About the Weather], 1865. In the issue of *Zvezda* for December 1929 and in the first three issues for 1930 a novella by Osip Mandel'štam entitled "Smert' Bozio" [The Death of Bosio] was announced for publication in 1930. Oddly enough, during all of 1929 the name had appeared as "Borgia," and that was also the spelling in the three succeeding issues for 1930. By the time of number 7 for 1930, however, no further announcement appeared, and the novella itself, if indeed it was ever completed, has never been printed. The concluding paragraphs of Chap. vii were published in quotation marks and are, probably, a part of the lost work. See the editorial note in Mandel'štam, *Sobranie sočinenij* [Collected Works], (New York, 1955), p. 392.

74. Annuška: It may be that Mandel'štam chose this name as a reference to the maid of his friend Georgij Ivanov, about whom Irina Odoevceva, Ivanov's wife, wrote in her recollections of Mandel'štam in *Novyj Žurnal* [The New Review], 71 (March 1963), 15.

75. "The Lord God might have given more brains and money": The line is from Pushkin's *Mednyj vsadnik* [The Bronze Horseman], 1, 35-36: "Čto mog by Bog emu pribavit'/ Uma i deneg" [That God might have given him more brains and money].

76. The original of this is an extended example of Mandel'štam's toponymic paronomasia: "Pod lebjaž'im, gagač'im, gagarinskim puxom—pod tučkovymi tučkami, pod francuzskim buše umirajuščix naberežnyx . . ." and so on. The Swan [*lebjažij*] Canal ran along the west side of the Summer Garden. The swan suggests down, which suggests the eider duck [*gaga*] from which down is commonly obtained, and the sound of this calls up Gagarin Street, not far from the Swan Canal and parallel to it. Gagarin Street leads into the French Embankment. Tučkov is the name of a bridge across the Little Neva. Other examples of this device are discussed above, p. 6of.

77. raspberries: There is an untranslatable play on the words "malina" [raspberries] and "malinnik" [raspberry patch] and Malinov, the name of the town.

Index of Names

NOTE: The transliteration in the index of names is that used in the notes (see A Note on Transliteration, p. vi). In those cases where confusion might result, both forms are cited, e.g., Akhmatova, Axmatova. The index includes all proper names, both of real and imagined persons.